W9-DHF-681

POLICY STUDIES IN EMPLOYMENT AND WELFARE NUMBER 12

General Editors: Sar A. Levitan and Garth L. Mangum

Upgrading Blue Collar and Service Workers

Charles Brecher

Foreword by Eli Ginzberg

The Johns Hopkins University Press, Baltimore and London

This report was prepared for the Manpower Administration, U.S. Department of Labor, under research contract Numbers 81–34–67–25 authorized by Title I of the Manpower Development and Training Act. Since contractors performing research under Government sponsorship are encouraged to express their own judgment freely, the report does not necessarily represent the Department's official opinion or policy. Moreover, the contractor is solely responsible for the factual accuracy of all material developed in the report.

Reproduction in whole or in part permitted for any purpose of the United States Government.

Copyright © 1972 by The Johns Hopkins University Press
All rights reserved
Manufactured in the United States of America

The Johns Hopkins University Press, Baltimore, Md. 21218
The Johns Hopkins Press Ltd., London

Library of Congress Catalog Card Number 79–186512

ISBN 0–8018–1411–1 (clothbound edition)
ISBN 0–8018–1401–4 (paperbound edition)

Originally published, 1972
Paperback edition, 1972

LIBRARY
FLORIDA STATE UNIVERSITY
TALLAHASSEE, FLORIDA

Contents

Acknowledgments

Dr. Eli Ginzberg, Director of the Conservation of Human Resources project, started me on this research effort and provided assistance at every stage. Several of my colleagues at the Conservation project also played a valuable role. Miriam Ostow was a continual source of information and suggestions. Marcia Freedman read over the manuscript and made comments which enabled me to improve it significantly.

William Johnson was my liaison at the New York City Rand Institute. He introduced me to a valuable data source and his consultations helped me utilize the available information in the most appropriate way.

I am indebted to the numerous employers, union representatives, and training program sponsors who gave freely of their time to discuss conditions in their industry with me. I have promised them anonymity, but without their cooperation the case studies would lack whatever depth they now have.

Ken Arnold served as editor and his work has made the book clearer in meaning and more relevant to the reader living outside of New York City. The author bears responsibility for all errors of fact and judgment.

Foreword

by Eli Ginzberg

These introductory pages are addressed to the following themes: the relations between manpower programming and upgrading; the principal findings emerging from Mr. Brecher's research; and policy recommendations.

From one point of view, all manpower programs aimed at improving the quality of the labor supply contain an upgrading component. In fact, since their primary objective is to add to the skills of workers with an aim of improving their job status and income, upgrading is the essence of manpower programming.

However, legislators and administrators have employed the term in a narrower context. They have restricted the concept of upgrading to training and related programs that are aimed at enabling employed workers to advance up the job hierarchy, either with their present employers or with others in the same or a different industry. However, there is no reason that the concept cannot include programs for unemployed persons who, as a result of training and other manpower services, will return to the labor force in a better position to get a better job.

These preliminary observations go only a short distance in clarifying the many difficulties inherent in the concept of upgrading as an objective of manpower programming. Let us note, at least briefly, some of the more intractable problems. There is, first, the basic structure of the job market or markets, which, without exception, have fewer good jobs at the top than indifferent and poor jobs at the bottom. Except in periods of high demand for skilled labor, the number of potential candidates for the better jobs exceeds by far the openings that are available.

It is well to remember that trade unions have long made it a primary goal of collective bargaining that the employer use objective criteria, such as seniority, for selecting workers for promotion. Without an objective system, scope for favoritism is given free reign and this, not unnaturally, leads to marked unrest in the work force.

Many workers can be upgraded only if they have the opportunity to add to their skills. In many cases, the employer, particularly the large employer, provides the training opportunities for those selected to be moved into more responsible positions. But training carries a cost. Employers are therefore careful to train only as many workers as they have openings. Moreover, they are careful to provide only enough training so that the worker can handle his new assignment effectively. To provide more would increase the probability that the worker will look around for a new job which would make use of his broadened competence and would pay more.

The labor market behaves quite differently in periods of expansion and contraction. In years of rapid growth, the opportunities for workers to advance into better jobs, i.e., to be upgraded, are much greater than when output and employment are stable or declining. In a recession, the opposite of upgrading often occurs: workers with more skill and more seniority bump workers with lesser skills. Many workers remain employed in a period of recession only by accepting a job for which they are overqualified and which pays less than the one they previously held. This phenomenon of downgrading during periods of slack activity decreases the amount of upgrading required when business improves. Many workers already have the skills required to move into more demanding assignments.

Additional trends in the labor market bear on upgrading. There is, first, the matter of arbitrary restrictions at point of entry or at transfer points in the job hierarchy. Through legal, administrative, and trade union arrangements the conditions of entry or advancement are frequently controlled. This means that the in-group is given preference for the good jobs that become available. Women, blacks, and other minority group members, and the poorly educated, tend to be frozen out.

A second development is the rapid shift in employment away from manufacturing in favor of the service sector. One concomitant of this shift is the much smaller size of the typical firm. As a consequence, there is less scope for intra-firm upgrading.

A third characteristic of the American economy is the extent to which workers, through job hopping, self-instruction, and other devices, are able to add to their skills and in the process improve their access to better jobs with higher pay. It is not usual to describe this type of labor market mobility as upgrading but, nevertheless, the worker-initiated, worker-directed process of skill acquisition and income improvement is perhaps the most important of all mobility routes.

These several considerations about the structure and operation of the labor market are some of the building blocks that Charles Brecher uses in his sharply focused investigation into the upgrading of blue collar and service workers in New York City in five major industries—apparel, food, health, construction, and transit. The scale of his inquiry is suggested by the fact that these five industries account for approximately 20 percent of total employment in New York City and for 50 percent of all non-white-collar employment.

By a judicious admixture of methods including industry studies, personal interviews with key leadership groups—employers, trade unions, educational and training officials—and through the analysis of Social Security earnings data for relevant groups of workers, Brecher has moved the discussion of upgrading from the ideological-moralistic plane of the New Careerists to the more mundane, analytical sphere of manpower economics. In the process, he has uncovered much of significance for an understanding of urban labor markets and manpower policy.

In brief review here are some of his more important generic findings, although we must note that each of the propositions outlined below does not hold for every one of the five industries and surely not to the same extent.

1. None of the industries has any real difficulty in filling its skilled jobs. For the most part they do this through upgrading within the organization or by adding skilled employees attached to the in-

dustry or attracted to the industry or attracted from other industries. Between three-quarters and four-fifths of all workers earning above $8,000 per year have been upgraded.

2. Formal training by employers for their more demanding positions
   is the exception rather than the rule. The supply of skilled
   workers is sufficiently large that employers have little difficulty
   in filling their openings.

3. In general, young people who pursue a vocational curriculum in
   high school do not learn enough to have a significant edge in
   obtaining employment in these industries and surely not for preferred access to skilled jobs.

4. On the other hand, those who pursue a vocational curriculum in
   community colleges, particularly if they acquire an A.A. degree
   and pass the certification or licensing requirement, are in a preferred position to obtain skilled jobs.

5. There is overwhelming evidence that women and minority group
   members are discriminated against when it comes to promotion
   into skilled jobs or entrance into training programs, particularly
   apprenticeship programs, that are a direct route to better jobs.
   Some headway is being made through the exercise of diverse
   pressures—political, legal, trade union—to remove some of the
   arbitrary barriers, but many remain.

6. Until recently—and then only selectively—trade unions have concentrated on obtaining higher wages, better fringe benefits, and
   better working conditions for their members rather than on en-
   couraging employers to initiate training programs to facilitate upgrading of the work force. The availability of federal funding to
   cover most of the costs of training—time lost plus instructional
   expenses—has led to some trade union interest in training for
   upgrading. But the subject remains relatively low on the agenda
   of most unions.

7. One of the severe constraints on upgrading is the success of established groups in restricting the pool of potential candidates for
   better jobs to those who meet certain arbitrary standards of education and work experience.

8. The costs of upgrading tend to be ignored or minimized. The
   most successful effort—the upgrading of nurses' aides to Licensed

Practical Nurses—involved an expenditure in excess of $6,000 per person.

9. An experimental and demonstration project using federal subsidies to encourage employers to upgrade their workers was delayed; the numbers involved are too small to permit definitive conclusions; but the thrust of this study is to raise serious questions about the potential of the subsidy approach. A small amount of money is not likely to result in considerable occupational restructuring. Yet until there is occupational restructuring, the opportunities for upgrading are likely to remain limited.

10. There is a shortage of part-time (late afternoon, evening, and Saturday) training opportunities under public auspices for workers who seek to add to their skills. While there is no convincing evidence to warrant a vast expansion of such training opportunities, some increase should prove helpful to ambitious workers who would be willing to trade leisure and carfare for an improved occupational future.

11. The advocates of the New Career approach have not taken adequate account of the head-on conflicts that will arise from their efforts to increase promotional opportunities for the less educated and less skilled with the limited number of good jobs that exist, the large numbers of competitors for these jobs, and the difficulties of removing the legal, administrative, and organizational impediments that currently control access to these jobs.

The author concludes that since powerful technological and economic factors make a substantial increase in upgrading impractical, attention should be directed to the following realistic and realizable goals: to increase the pool of eligibles who are considered for upgrading and to improve the selection mechanism. At a minimum, this would be a gain for equity although it would not significantly improve the efficiency of the labor market. Brecher's other principal recommendation in view of the inherent limitations of programs aimed at upgrading is in line with trade union policy: to seek to improve the wages and working conditions of employees at the lower end of the occupational hierarchy.

In this concluding section, we will consider what this study can contribute to manpower policy beyond the subjects adumbrated above.

For some time critics have charged that the administrators of man-power programs have not paid sufficient attention to the legislative stress on upgrading. This study suggests that the error may be with the legislative intent, not with the administrators' recalcitrance. If the opportunities for upgrading are as limited as they appear to be, new comprehensive manpower legislation should reflect these limitations.

A recurring theme considered by manpower specialists has been the relation between the strenuous governmental efforts to find places for the hard-to-employ in the economy and the correlative necessity of providing for the upgrading of those who now hold entrance jobs. Their formulation has been that unless those who now occupy the least desirable positions can advance a step or two, there will be no room at the bottom for the hard-to-employ. Several observations suggest themselves. Room has in fact been found for a large number of the hard-to-employ. However, many drop out within the first six or twelve months after they have been hired. Among the many reasons for such a high dropout rate is the correct perception of many hard-to-employ that their opportunities for advancement are seriously limited.

The facts are these: upgrading those in low level jobs is never easy and becomes difficult in periods of recession. Yet without some reasonable, improved mobility for those already on payrolls, the number of places available for the hard-to-employ will be limited, and of those who are hired, many will become discouraged and quit when they see no opportunity for moving up.

The situation is exacerbated in the case of many young blacks whose expectations have been raised to a point where they balk at accepting a dead-end job. But many jobs are dead-end in one sense of the term; there is no opportunity for advancement within the firm. However, many of these jobs are not necessarily dead-end because skill accumulation can be built on intra-industry and inter-industry mobility. But since employment discrimination is rampant, many young blacks feel that their prospects of building a successful occupational career on job and industry mobility will prove difficult if not impossible. So they give up in despair.

During the last years, trade unions have penetrated the service sector of the economy, and this in turn has brought about some rationalization of the occupational structure and the opening up of more opportunities for the promotion of workers at the lower end of the hierarchy. Some additional gains can be expected from the twin push of unionization and larger organizational units. More importantly, these developments, together with increasing public awareness of the number of workers who are unable to support their families even though they work full-time, full-year, may presage a relative improvement in the wages and working conditions of those at the bottom of the scale.

We need more aggressive public action to remove racial and other types of discriminatory barriers to employment and promotion. No single line of action promises as much relief to the peripheral member of society and the labor force as effective action on this front. But even if this long overdue effort is energetically pursued and succeeds, tensions will arise between better educated white women and less educated minority group members, both men and women.

The fact that there is no easy way to assure access to better jobs for the entire population should not obscure the desirability of public efforts to expand and improve training opportunities so that those who want to improve their employment status are not blocked because of an inability to add to their skills. Community colleges open to those without degrees and federally funded skill training centers represent two important advances. But the scale and scope of adult vocational training must be broadened and deepened if those who most need opportunity can have it.

Finally, attention must be called to the one condition that will nullify most of the foregoing efforts unless it is remedied. The critical factor in upgrading, as in most other aspects of manpower programming and policy, is the level of employment. Unless there are jobs for all who are able and willing to work, manpower efforts, especially those directed to the disadvantaged, will be wasted. The United States has been experimenting for one decade with manpower training. At best the results have been mixed. In the decade that lies ahead, the United States must move energetically to build the capability of providing jobs whenever there is a shortfall of demand in the private sector. And it must do more: it must learn how to provide jobs that tap the developed competences of people and provide them opportunities for adding to their competences. Only then will we have the foundations for an effective upgrading policy.

1

Upgrading: Concept and Issues

Upgrading is a concept which generates confusion. When the United States Department of Labor sponsored a conference to discuss the topic in 1970, those in attendance could not establish whether the invited papers were to consider upgrading, or new careers, or both—or whether the phrases referred to an identical phenomenon. With such misunderstanding over the nature of the concept it is not surprising that the conference participants differed significantly over its importance. Some considered it a vital aspect of all future manpower programs while others seemed to view the idea as little more than a hoax.[1] The most useful conclusion one can extract from previous discussions of upgrading is that there is no general agreement on the subject.

THE CONCEPT OF UPGRADING

There is no precise definition of the term "upgrading" as it applies to manpower policies. What most people have in mind when they use the word is the movement of an individual from one job to a second job which is considered "better" for one or more reasons. But this common-sense definition needs refinement, for it covers too wide a variety of

---

[1] National Manpower Policy Task Force, *Conference on Upgrading and New Careers* (Washington: National Manpower Policy Task Force, 1970).

1

labor market behaviors. How does upgrading differ from a promotion? How does it differ from a complete change of vocation?

For clarification, the concept should be analyzed in the context of the various dimensions of labor mobility. One may remain in the labor force and yet move in many ways. A worker can change the geographic area in which he works (geographic mobility), the industry in which he works (interindustry mobility), the specific set of tasks he performs (occupational mobility), the amount of money he earns (earnings mobility), and/or the firm in which he works (employer mobility).

It would be convenient if upgrading could be defined as a unique combination of the above elements, but we are not so fortunate. We can suggest that a worker not be considered upgraded unless he experiences some raise in pay level, but on occasion a worker considers himself upgraded even though he is not getting more money. The young secretary who moves from a dreary two-girl office in a garment shop to a larger and more luxurious company headquarters populated with male co-workers may consider herself to be in a better job even if the pay is not higher. In most cases, however, upgrading entails a wage increase. It also should involve movement into a position consisting of tasks requiring greater skill or responsibility. However, Marcia Freedman has pointed to several forms of internal labor market mobility which do not require greater skill or responsibility, such as pay increments for seniority and job shifts resulting from organizational changes.[2] Upgrading usually does not entail geographic mobility, but it may. The salesman who is transferred from a low yield territory to a larger and more prosperous one considers himself upgraded because of the added responsibility and income.

Depending upon the occupational clusters involved, upgrading may or may not require interindustry mobility. In most blue collar and service fields occupations are industry specific, and a change in industry means the worker is changing his entire career pattern rather than upgrading himself. Some occupational sequences, notably those of professionals and clerical workers, are found in various industries, and up-

---

[2]Marcia Freedman, *The Process of Work Establishment* (New York: Columbia University Press, 1960).

grading can take place along with movement from one industry to another. With all these limitations and reservations in mind we may define upgrading as a (positive) change in earnings associated with a shift to an occupation composed of tasks of increased skill or responsibility, usually not requiring a change in location or industry, which may or may not require a change of employer.

The concept of upgrading may also be clarified by considering it in the context of the theory of internal labor markets, most recently analyzed by Michael Piore and Peter Doeringer.[3] They define an internal labor market as an administrative unit within which labor is allocated by institutional rules. Typically, the administrative unit is a single private business firm, but it may be a governmental agency or a division of a larger corporation. The theoretical internal labor market consists of two types of jobs: those filled by workers from the external or conventional labor market (ports of entry), and those filled by workers previously employed in the firm.

Internal labor markets vary in their structure. Some plants may hire from external sources for almost every job classification. Others hire outsiders for only a few positions and fill the remaining jobs, which usually require higher skill levels, through promotions. The most important factors motivating employers to fill positions internally are necessity and efficiency. Some jobs require information and skills which can only be obtained by experience in the plant. Many skills can be acquired only through practice or proximity to other jobs. In such cases workers with experience in the plant are the only ones qualified for skilled positions. Internal staffing tends to be efficient because the worker produces as he learns, the employer has a pool of available workers from which to draw, and the individual learns at a pace tailored to his ability and the requisite skills. In addition it is probable that the use of internal sources reduces turnover in lower-level positions.

The structure of internal labor markets has important implications for training institutions. It determines which skills the employer himself will develop in his employees and which skills he will rely upon

[3] *Work Force Adjustments in Private Industry—Their Implications for Manpower Policy* (Washington: U.S. Dept. of Labor, Manpower Automation Research Monograph no. 7, October 1968).

formal training institutions to develop. Thus, there are two related determinations an employer must make. What preparation or training a worker must have to qualify for a position and whether workers should be recruited internally or externally. When a job requires skills that can only be learned through work experience in the plant, he has no option. However, cases in the real world are rarely so clear-cut, and employers may recruit labor from similar firms with related skill requirements or hire unskilled workers and give them special training. When no special skills are required for a position, the employer may rely upon internal or external sources. However, unskilled jobs are usually low-paying jobs. Employed workers are likely to be compensated already at levels equal to or higher than those of unskilled jobs and will not move into these positions. Consequently, most unskilled jobs are filled from the external labor market.

Positions requiring formal preparation are likely to be filled by those in the external labor market who have recently completed their period of study. Employers may also select some of their own workers for subsidized training and subsequently promote them. Although this is not a common practice, some large organizations do send workers to school in order to qualify them for an advanced position. Other firms may hire over-qualified workers at lower levels and thereby have an internal supply of formally qualified workers from which to select. For example, publishers frequently hire female college graduates to perform secretarial chores because they believe they may eventually advance them to editorial positions. Both cases illustrate the fact that the need for formal training does not rule out the use of internal labor sources.

Upgrading, in the context of the internal labor market, generally refers to one of two phenomena. The first is the ongoing process described above. Unskilled workers are hired at ports of entry. Through work experience and observation they acquire skills needed for better paying jobs. When vacancies occur the employer fills them with the experienced worker. The employee has been upgraded. Upgrading may also refer to a special effort made by a firm to fill intermediate and higher level positions from the ranks of unskilled workers. A special effort may be required when the informal skill acquisition process described earlier is not sufficient to equip an unskilled worker for the better job. When this informal or "natural" process is not operating, an employer may create special trainee positions or training classes for employees to enable them to function in better paying jobs. Upgrading may thus refer to both an ongoing or natural process which exists within many firms and to special efforts made by employers to enable their unskilled workers to qualify for more advanced positions. In both cases the result is a promotion; that is, the worker moves from one job to another within the firm.

The meaning of upgrading in the context of internal labor market theory differs from the definition derived from a consideration of the dimensions of labor mobility. In the former case, it is limited to occupational advancement within a single firm. In the latter case, advancement is not restricted to a single firm but may result from movement between employers.

In this study the difference is reconciled by altering the concept of an internal labor market. Rather than restricting it to a single administrative unit we shall consider each local service or manufacturing industry as an internal labor market. The rules for allocating labor within the internal labor market are no longer set exclusively by administrative regulations, but are established by custom and practice in the industry as well. Ports of entry may be defined as positions open to those without prior experience in the industry. Positions filled internally are those restricted to workers with experience in the industry, regardless of whether this experience is with the particular firm. In this context the firm, or the traditional internal labor market, is only one setting within which upgrading may take place. Workers may also advance by changing employers.

The distinction may be clarified through an example from a service industry with which many readers are likely to be familiar—higher education. Consider the selection of a department chairman at a university. The position might be filled by a professor in the same university. The individual would probably have acquired some of the requisite administrative and diplomatic skills through an informal process of observation and experience. In this case the position could be considered as filled by upgrading under both definitions of the term. However, the position might also be filled by a professor from another university. He, too, might have acquired the needed skills in an informal manner. If one uses the usual single firm model of an internal labor market in this case, the position of department chairman is a port of entry. If one views the industry as an internal labor market, the promotion remains an internal one since the new incumbent has had experience in the relevant lower level position in the industry.

The difference between firm and industry definitions of an internal labor market may not always be significant. In many cases an area has only one firm in a particular industry. There may be only one large plant in each of the several manufacturing industries located in a town. For some service industries it is quite likely that all local police, sanitation, education, and other social services will be provided by one monopolistic employer, usually a public agency. In such cases all intra-industry advancement necessarily takes place within one administrative unit. In large metropolitan areas or in industries characterized by numerous small firms the distinction becomes important. In such cases workers may advance by moving from one firm to another within the industry. Mobility should be analyzed in the context of the industry in order to consider the potential for this type of advancement.

THE ISSUES

If upgrading is viewed as a process of intra-industry occupational mobility, what are the research and policy issues that should be explored? Relatively few workers have what can be considered a "good" job. According to national census figures only slightly over 15 percent of all workers earned more than $10,000 in 1969,[4] a year when the Bureau of Labor Statistics estimated it required $10,077 for an urban family to live at a moderate level. The key issue is how these better jobs are filled. No nation has an economy which permits all its workers to be chiefs and none Indians. We can hope to have a society in which the better jobs are not reserved for a selected few. The purpose of up-

---

[4]U.S. Bureau of the Census, *Current Population Reports*, series P-60, no. 75, "Income in 1969 of Families and Persons in the United States" (Washington, D.C., 1970).

grading is to insure some access to "good" (or at least better) jobs for those who occupy low wage positions. Research dealing with upgrading should focus on the way in which the better jobs are filled.

Extant literature provides some clues about the incidence of upgrading in the United States and the significance of training in the process. Occupational mobility has long been of interest to both economists and sociologists. From the studies these scholars have undertaken it is possible to sketch the broad outlines of the process by which men reach the higher levels of the occupational structure.

Data from Blau and Duncan's study of *The American Occupational Structure*,[5] and similar data gathered by researchers at Ohio State University under the direction of Herbert Parnes,[6] indicate that for all nonagricultural occupations a majority of the workers did not begin their careers in their present position. Professionals are more likely than any other nonagricultural group to have begun in their present occupation, primarily because of the extended educational preparation required. Even so, a majority of professionals moved into their present position from another occupation. Only a small percentage of those in sales positions began working in this type of job, and only about one craftsman in ten started at his present level. Workers moving up the occupational ladder are an important source of manpower for many higher level positions.

The same studies show that while many workers in better jobs have moved up, their advancement has generally been limited. For example, most of those moving into professional positions had their first fulltime job after leaving school in other white collar positions while relatively few began as laborers or operatives. Similarly, more manufacturing craftsmen began as manufacturing operatives than as any other type of worker. It is true that most men have moved up into their current job, but the move is likely to have been a limited one.

[5] Peter M. Blau and Otis Dudley Duncan, *The American Occupational Structure* (New York: John Wiley and Sons, 1967).

[6] Herbert Parnes, *et. al., The Pre-Retirement Years* (Washington: U.S. Department of Labor, Manpower Research Monograph no. 15, 1970), pp. 116–32. See also, Gladys Palmer, *Labor Mobility in Six Cities* (New York: Social Science Research Council, 1954).

Few occupations are filled with a significant number of workers who have moved downward into their current job. Using a detailed index to rank occupational titles, the Parnes study cited above found that only 16 percent of all men between the ages of 45 and 59 moved downward to their present position. Like upward mobility, this downward mobility tends to be limited. For example, professionals shifting occupations tend to move into other white collar occupations; they accounted for more than 10 percent of the nonretail salesmen but less than 1 percent of the laborers.

A study by the Bureau of Labor Statistics provides some indication of the ways in which occupational mobility takes place.[7] The study found that 9.3 percent of the work force had changed occupations during 1965. Of this group 82 percent of the males also shifted employers, and 71 percent changed the industry in which they worked. The figures for females were 88 percent and 77 percent, respectively. From these data we can infer that about 15 percent of all occupational moves are promotions, demotions, or lateral moves within a single firm. Approximately 10 percent are moves in which an employee shifts firms but not the industry in which he works. Both of these types of moves are likely to be along a sequence of related jobs; they take place within what we have called an internal labor market. The remaining 75 percent of all occupational shifts involve changes of both employer and industry. It is not likely that many of these changes are moves which fall within our definition of upgrading. Most of the inter-industry occupational shifts were among the lower skilled, blue collar categories. When these workers change their industry, they tend to do so involuntarily because of layoffs and other reasons. Lowell Gallaway's analysis of inter-industry mobility, using social security data from the years 1957 to 1960, found that male workers remaining in the same industry over the period had annual earnings averaging $1,820 above those who shifted industries. This relationship was true for every major industry group except agriculture.[8] A survey of individuals changing jobs in

[7] Samuel Saben, "Occupational Mobility of Employed Workers," Special Labor Force Report no. 84.

[8] Lowell Gallaway, *Interindustry Labor Mobility in the United States, 1957-1960.* (Washington: Social Security Administration, Research Report no. 18, 1967).

1961 found that only approximately one-third did so in order to improve their status. The majority of job changes were due to layoffs and other related reasons.[9] Neither the Gallaway study nor the 1961 survey was concerned exclusively with inter-industry occupational shifts, but the findings of both provide evidence that much of this type of mobility is involuntary.

While studies support the conclusion that upgrading is an ongoing process in American industry and that many of those in better jobs have moved up from lower levels, they also reveal that many workers do not have a chance to advance. The Parnes study cited above found that 13 percent of the men were in the same specific occupation in which they began their careers and that another 16 percent experienced only a lateral move involving no gain in socio-economic status.

Occupational inertia would not be a serious problem if it were confined to those at the upper levels of the occupational hierarchy. But this is not the case. Blau and Duncan's study showed that more than one of every five nonfarm laborers has been in his present position throughout his working life, and the figure is even higher for operatives. Their calculations indicated that those remaining in the same occupation are over-represented at the lower levels and that more than one-third of all those not changing occupation during their careers were operatives, service workers, or laborers.

The major barriers to advancement which have been identified are race, education, and training. Negroes have been prevented from participating in the process of upward occupational mobility on an equal basis with whites. Blau and Duncan's comprehensive study of statistical evidence concluded that race was an independent factor affecting the prospects for mobility. They summarized their findings as follows:

A Negro's chances of occupational success in the United States are far inferior to those of a Caucasian. Whereas this hardly comes as a surprise to anyone familiar with the American scene, it is noteworthy that Negroes are handicapped at every step in their attempts to achieve economic success, and these cumulative disadvantages are what produce the great inequalities of opportunities under which the Negro American

[9] Gertrude Bancroft and Stuart Garfinkle, "Job Mobility in 1961," Special Labor Force Report no. 35.

suffers. Disproportionate numbers of Negroes live in the South, where occupational opportunities are not so great as in the North. Within each region, moreover, Negroes are seriously disadvantaged. They have lower social origins than whites, and they receive less education. Even when Negroes and Whites with the same amount of education are compared, Negroes enter the job market on lower levels. Furthermore, if all these differences are statistically controlled and we ask how Negroes would fare if they had the same origins, education and career beginnings as whites, the chances of occupational achievement are still considerably inferior to those of whites.[10]

Innumerable studies have found education to be significantly correlated in a positive fashion with occupational status and income. In addition, education is related to job training. The Department of Labor's survey of occupational training among American workers showed that nearly two-thirds of those who had received formal training had graduated from high school and that nearly 70 percent of those without training had not.[11] Ivar Berg's recent study, *Education and Jobs*, demonstrates that both public and private employers use educational achievement as a criterion for hiring and promoting workers and that educational requirements for many jobs have been raised in recent years, even though there is no objective evidence showing that education and job performance are related.[12] Whether their practices are rational or not, employers rely upon educational preparation as a means for selecting personnel for jobs and for training programs. The result of these practices is that those who lack the proper education and training are most likely to be confined to the lower levels of the occupational structure.

Policy initiatives to develop upgrading opportunities have focused on overcoming the barriers to advancement presented by a lack of education and training. Research and demonstration projects have been funded to test the suitability of alternative training arrangements ranging from in-plant training provided during working hours to classroom instruction at outside institutions during the workers' free time.

[10] Blau and Duncan, *American Occupational Structure*, pp. 404–405.

[11] *Formal Occupational Training of Adult Workers* (Washington: U.S. Dept. of Labor, Manpower/Automation Research Monograph no. 2, 1964).

[12] Ivar Berg, *Education and Jobs* (New York: Praeger, 1970).

The impetus for training to facilitate upgrading came from the research which accompanied the war on poverty. It was "discovered" that many of those whom the government defined as poor were working full-time. The most recent (1969) data show that 22 percent of the nearly five million families in the United States living in poverty have a head of the household who works full-time all year, and in earlier years the figure has exceeded 30 percent.[13] The phenomenon of underemployment contradicted the popular notion that the way out of poverty was a job, and highlighted the need to help individuals qualify for better jobs so that they would not be confined to low paying jobs for their entire working lives. If so many of the poor are already hard at work, then it is believed that what is needed is assistance to help them advance to higher wage positions. Consequently the underemployed were added to the unemployed as a target group for manpower programs. This approach has also been incorporated into welfare reform proposals which make the working poor eligible for assistance and which attempt to provide recipients with training or temporary public service jobs which will eventually lead to more rewarding positions.

The present thrust of upgrading policy is to train workers so that they can move into higher wage positions. The latest *Manpower Report of the President* presented the objectives as follows:

An upgrading program should do two things for employed workers. It should improve their job skills—and often their ability to cope with the environmental problems which affect work capability. Secondly, it should produce, in a reasonably brief period, an increase in earnings through advancement to higher paid jobs or more stable employment.[14]

The purpose of this study is to explore the potential of increased public expenditure to facilitate upgrading of unskilled workers. The prior research outlined earlier has established that upgrading is an ongoing practice in American industry. The key questions are: Can government intervention be utilized to increase the opportunities for up-

---

[13] U.S. Bureau of the Census, *Current Population Reports*, series P-60, no. 76, "24 Million Americans—Poverty in the United States: 1969" (Washington, D.C., 1970), Table 14; and U.S. Bureau of the Census, *Current Population Reports*, series P-60, no. 68, "Poverty in the United States: 1959 to 1968" (Washington, D.C., 1969), Table 8.

[14] *Manpower Report of the President*, April 1970, pp. 49–50.

ward mobility among low income workers? If so, what forms of intervention are likely to be most effective and how many workers can be reached successfully? In short, what is the potential for improving upgrading practices through public action?

DESIGN OF THIS STUDY

This exploratory effort consists of five case studies of selected industries in New York City. The five industries are apparel manufacturing, health services, food services, construction, and local public transit. The New York City labor market is characterized by the multiple problems which upgrading is intended to alleviate. Its labor force consists of a relatively large percentage of minority group workers (18 percent Negro and 9 percent Puerto Rican). Underemployment is a far more serious problem than unemployment in the city's economy. The New York State Department of Labor estimated that in New York City in 1969 unemployment averaged about 130,000 during the year. In the same year over 242,000 individuals were employed full-time but had family incomes below a poverty line set at $3,300 for a family of four. About 150,000 individuals worked full-time and were classified as near-poor, a category with a maximum income of $4,345 for a family of four.[15]

The industries were chosen for a variety of reasons. Apparel manufacturing is the largest single manufacturing industry in the city and provides employment for over 200,000 people. Health services is another large industry in the city, and it has experienced rapid growth with about 50,000 new jobs emerging in the last decade to bring current employment levels to about 200,000. Like apparel manufacturing it is viewed as an important source of jobs for the minority community.

Contract construction was selected because of the widely held belief that it represents a potential source of high wage jobs for minority groups of which they have not always been able to take advantage. The food service industry is a source of employment for about 170,000 workers and represents the service sector of the economy. Finally, local

---

[15] New York State Department of Labor, "Annual Manpower Planning Report, Fiscal Year 1971, New York, New York."

public transit represents a traditional public service, as distinct from the newer human services (health, education, welfare) and one for which government officials are contemplating a resurgence of growth. Its civil service status has made it a desirable source of steady employment. Coincidentally, during the period of the study, the New York City transit system experienced increased operating difficulties which some critics attributed to manpower problems. Together the five industries represent a total of approximately 800,000 jobs out of a total New York City work force of 4.1 million.

Various sources of data were used to develop the case studies. In each case a review of the relevant literature, including Department of Labor surveys, was supplemented with interviews with knowledgeable individuals having direct contact with the industry. The individuals were selected with an eye toward their being able to lead the investigator to another, and in every case employers, representatives of employer organizations, and/or union officials were contacted. Interviews were also conducted with the sponsors of a variety of training programs operating in the city, and visits were made to several of these institutions.

The interviews were analyzed along with data extracted from the New York metropolitan area subsample of the Social Security Administration's national work history file. This subsample was developed by the New York City Rand Institute, and the interested reader can find a detailed description of its contents in a recent Rand publication.[16] Because reference will be made to data from the sample in the case studies, however, a brief summary of the file's characteristics is presented here and six important, but somewhat technical, limitations of the data file are listed in the appendix to this chapter. The file is a one percent sample of all workers who were employed by firms in the metropolitan area which are covered by Social Security regulations during the period 1962 to 1966. The principal exclusions are government employment and private railroad employees, which accounts for the absence of data on local public transit employees. The subsample

[16]William Johnson, *Changing Patterns of Employment in the New York Metropolitan Area* (New York: New York City Rand Institute, forthcoming).

contains estimates of annual income for workers based upon their payments to the Social Security fund. For high income individuals only estimates are possible, but for most of the employees covered in this study the income data are quite accurate. Additional data in the file include age, sex, and race of each employee and the industry in which he earned most of his annual income.

The principal advantage of the Social Security file is that it is continuous. The same individuals are followed each year. This enables us to determine what percent of an industry's workforce remains in the industry over a specified period (1962–1966) and how much their income has increased as a result of this attachment.

The case studies will provide specific information about the way in which better jobs are filled in each of the five industries. In addition, because they represent a variety of industrial settings, the case studies should provide a sound basis for more general conclusions regarding the potential for upgrading programs and the directions they should take.

Appendix

The Rand Corporation's New York metropolitan area subsample of the Social Security Administration's continuous work history sample file is a useful source of information, but the reader should keep in mind the following facts about the data source:

1. Individuals working for employers not covered by Social Security provisions will not be counted as employed in the file.

2. Earnings exempt from Social Security regulations, such as much income received in the form of gratuities, will not be included in the estimated total income.

3. Estimated annual income refers to earnings from all sources of employment, while industry of employment refers to the largest segment of total income.

4. The total employment in an industry includes all people who worked during the year and had that industry as their largest single source of income. This differs from the usual Department of Labor survey definition of employment, which counts only those employed in the industry at a specified moment in time.

5. The file contains no occupational information, and occupational status can only be inferred from the industry and earnings data.

6. All information relating to geographic location refers to the individual's place of employment and not his place of residence.

2

Apparel Manufacture

OVERVIEW OF THE INDUSTRY

The manufacture of apparel and related products, usually referred to as the garment industry, is the largest manufacturing industry in New York City. In 1970 the industry provided an average of about 204,000 jobs in the city. As with most other manufacturing industries, the garment industry has been leaving New York City in order to find the space required for expansion and modernization and to tap new sources of lower wage labor. The result of this movement has been an absolute net decline in the city of approximately 64,000 jobs over the past decade.[1] Since the industry has grown nationally, New York's decline has had a magnified impact on the city's importance in the field. Since 1960 the city's share has decreased from almost 22 percent to only about 15 percent of total employment in the garment industry in the United States.

Employment in the garment industry is distributed unevenly among different types of firms and among producers of several types of clothing.[2] The three kinds of firms are manufacturers, contractors, and

[1] Bureau of Labor Statistics, *Changing Patterns of Prices, Pay, Workers, and Work on the New York Scene*, Regional Report no. 20, May, 1971.

[2] An excellent analysis of the industry is Ray B. Helfgott, "Women's and Children's Apparel," in *Made in New York: Case Studies in Metropolitan Manufacturing*, ed. Max Hall (Cambridge: Harvard University Press, 1951), pp. 19–134.

16

jobbers. Manufacturers perform all the functions necessary to produce a garment within their own shop. They design clothes, prepare samples, cut the cloth, sew the garments, and sell the finished products to retailers. Jobbers perform only entrepreneurial functions. They produce samples, buy material, and market the designs, but arrange for contractors to do the production work. Contractors work on material owned by jobbers and sew the garments according to designs they are given. In New York City the jobber-contractor relationship prevails and there are few manufacturers. Some New York jobbers send cut material to contractors located in lower wage areas outside the city. Most of the firms are small, with jobbers usually employing fewer individuals than contractors, and contractors fewer than manufacturers.

When considered by product, employment in the industry is unevenly distributed among several specialized fields. The largest segment is women's and misses' dresses and coats, which together constitute almost half the entire industry. Another large component is men's and boys' clothing (15 percent). The remainder of the workers are spread out among manufacturers of women's and children's underwear, hats and millinery, children's outerwear, and other miscellaneous products.

While the occupational structure of each specific segment of the industry varies, the composition of the two largest subsets is outlined in two recent surveys of firms in New York City (see Table 2.1).

In all segments of the industry the sewing operations account for the largest number of employees. In both women's and men's wear, over half the production employees are engaged in this type of occupation. Hand sewers are used to finish off parts of garments and to attach selected pieces such as trim or buttons to the clothing. Sewing machine operators work under either a tailor or section system. In the tailor system, which is frequently found in women's dress shops, one operator produces most of the garment. In the section system an operator is responsible for only one operation in the production process, such as attaching a sleeve or collar. This system is used extensively for men's wear and is also found in some women's shops. The piecework method of compensation is used for most sewers and machine operators, so that earnings vary with the individual's proficiency. Average hourly wages tend to be higher for tailor system operators than for other sewers.

17

Table 2.1 Characteristics of Selected Occupations in Two Apparel Manufacturing Industries

	Women's and Misses' Dresses			Men's & Boys' Suits & Coats		
	Percent of Total	Percent Female	Average Hourly Wage	Percent of Total	Percent Female	Average Hourly Wage
Total – all production workers	100.0%	72.5%	$3.27	100.0%	48.5%	$2.68
Selected Occupations						
cutters, markers	7.6	0.0	4.28	6.9	0.0	3.54
inspectors	2.1	97.7	2.31	1.2	51.1	2.20
pressers[a]	6.8	8.1	5.70	12.2	3.1	3.16
hand sewers	9.4	97.0	2.64	16.5	81.3	2.29
machine operators (section)	7.2	95.9	2.75	34.5	58.3	2.86
machine operators (tailor)	38.1	95.6	3.46	–	–	–
thread trimmers	3.6	98.5	2.11	2.8	97.9	1.78
work distributors	.1	89.5	2.07	.9	36.4	1.69

[a]includes underpressers in Men's and Boys' Suits and Coats.

SOURCES: U.S. Dept. of Labor, Bureau of Labor Statistics, *Industry Wage Survey, Men's and Boys' Suits and Coats, April, 1967*, Bulletin No. 1594, Table 15; and U.S. Dept. of Labor, Bureau of Labor Statistics, *Industry Wage Survey, Women's and Misses' Dresses, August, 1968*, Bulletin No. 1649, Table 12.

Other occupational groups account for smaller numbers. The related jobs of cutters, markers, and spreaders, which together constitute about 7 percent of the workforce, are of individuals responsible for laying out the material, marking it according to pattern and size, and cutting it properly. They are paid relatively high wages, with compensation in women's shops averaging more than in men's. Pressers are usually paid on a piecework basis and comprise about 7 percent of the production workers in women's shops and a somewhat higher percent in men's shops where underpressers are used in the production process as well as pressers who work on the finished garments. Most of the remaining production workers are in occupations of small size such as trimmers and inspectors who clean and check the finished pieces of clothing. There are also individuals in shipping and packing operations. Most of these employees are paid on an hourly basis at wage rates only slightly above the statutory minimum. As Table 2.1 indicates, the wage scale has a wide range, varying from about $1.70 per hour for distributors in men's wear to $5.70 per hour for pressers in women's wear shops.

OCCUPATIONAL MOBILITY

Advancement patterns in the industry are different for men and for women. Women are hired primarily as operators and for a few of the related production jobs such as trimmers and inspectors. While there is a sizeable proportion of male operators in the men's clothing segment of the industry, most operators in other parts of the industry are female. These jobs, which tend to be low wage, are the only positions open to females. One may increase one's earnings by increasing speed on the machine, which will yield higher earnings under the piecework system. However, there are no significant avenues for occupational mobility open to women. Positions as machine operators are entry jobs which lead to practically no promotional positions. Occasionally operators may be advanced to floorlady or supervisory positions, but frequently a good operator can make more on a piecework basis than a floorlady does on an hourly basis.

The very limited advancement opportunities for females are evident in the social security data. (See Table 2.2.) In 1962 over 75 percent of all females working in the garment industry earned less than $3,000, and another 21 percent earned between $3,000 and $5,000. It is impossible to determine how many of these individuals worked part-time, but the majority are probably full-time, part-year workers. Employment in the industry is seasonal. National figures indicate that the garment industry has a smaller percentage of its labor force working full-time, full-year than any other manufacturing industry and than most service industries. Despite the low earnings and seasonal employment a large majority of the workers remain in the industry for at least four years. As Table 2.2 indicates, approximately 60 percent of all females working in the garment industry in 1962 were also working in the industry in 1966. For those earning between $3,000 and $5,000 in 1962 the figure was over 75 percent, and for those earning between $2,000 and $3,000 it was 69 percent.

19

Table 2.2   The 1966 Status of Workers in the New York City Garment Industry
in 1962 by Their 1962 Income

1962 Income	FEMALES			MALES		
	Percent of all Workers	Percent in Same Industry in 1966	Percent of Stayers Moving Up	Percent of all Workers	Percent in Same Industry in 1966	Percent of Stayers Moving Up
$1-999	23%	31%	65%	13%	18%	82%
1,000-1,999	25	56	59	10	35	51
2,000-2,999	28	69	38	12	44	63
3,000-3,999	15	77	34	13	60	53
4,000-4,999	6	76	34	11	81	69
5,000-5,999	2	76	43	9	78	66
6,000-6,999	1	81	46	8	73	49
7,000-7,999	1	92	46	7	83	54
8,000-8,999	*	100	20	4	83	54
9,000-9,999	*	100	*	3	71	59
10,000-14,999	*	75	67	6	75	17
15,000 & over	*	50	*	4	77	*
Total - percent	100	59	45	100	60	53
- number	2,478	1,466	660	1,161	691	368

*denotes less than one-half of one percent

These high attachment rates are not explained by favorable advancement opportunities. A relatively small proportion of the 1962 workers who continued to work in the industry in 1966 moved up at least one step on the income scale in Table 2.2. (In all cases but the last two this represents an average increase of $1,000 in annual earnings over the four-year period. Since during the same period average weekly earnings of production workers in manufacturing in New York City rose $12.09, or an annual total of $629, a gain of $1,000 is likely to indicate some occupational advancement.) Because of the seasonal nature of the industry, it is possible that some workers achieved income gains of $1,000 or more by moving into more stable employment and raising the number of hours they worked during the year without necessarily experiencing occupational mobility. For the industry as a whole about 45 percent of the females remaining in the industry moved up the income scale, but in the $2,000 to $4,999 categories the same figure ranged between 34 percent and 38 percent.

The garment industry does not appear to be a promising field for females. Most of the jobs provide a low annual income and few chances for advancement. Yet a high proportion of the workers stay in the industry. Two possible explanations come to mind. It may be that the alternatives to employment in the garment industry are worse, or there may be benefits other than wages or potential advancement which attract the workers. The possible benefits related to employment in a garment shop are not great. Physical working conditions tend to be poor. The work is seasonal and unstable, but to some females this may be an advantage since it provides an opportunity to alternate periods of work and leisure, during which some income is provided by unemployment insurance. The best explanation is probably the limited employment alternatives for women who lack white-collar skills. Of those females who left the industry, well over half reported no earnings in 1966, which indicates they left the labor force because of inadequate work opportunities or because they had to assume full-time family responsibilities. Only about 10 percent of the industry's 1962 female labor force was working in another industry in New York City in 1966, and only 55 percent of this small group moved up the income scale at least one step. Women appear to remain in the garment industry despite the low wages because of the paucity of alternative opportunities.

For males the occupational distribution and the opportunities for advancement are more promising. Although males are found in many low-wage positions, including some operative jobs and most shipping and packing jobs, they also fill most of the better paying jobs, such as pressers, cutters, markers, and spreaders. In addition the small administrative and sales segment of the industry is composed primarily of males. There are opportunities for upward mobility. Positions as cutters and markers are usually filled by men recruited either by relatives or from promising male employees in lower level positions. They spend anywhere from six months to several years assisting and observing the skilled men. Through informal on-the-job training they learn to spread material, lay out the patterns, mark the goods and cut them. Positions as pressers are more likely to be ports of entry; new recruits are quickly trained on the job, or begin as underpressers and then become finishing pressers.

Table 2.3   Characteristics of Workers Employed in the New York City Garment Industry in 1966 by Their 1966 Income

Income in 1966	Percent of all Workers	Percent also in Industry in 1962	Percent Upgraded since 1962	Percent Female	Percent Negro
$1-999	18%	32%	*	80%	19%
1,000-1,999	15	51	7	83	17
2,000-2,999	21	63	26	86	18
3,000-3,999	16	69	40	81	17
4,000-4,999	9	76	50	66	20
5,000-5,999	5	78	57	45	11
6,000-6,999	4	75	52	35	6
7,000-7,999	3	77	56	28	4
8,000-8,999	2	83	59	9	6
9,000-9,999	1	82	55	8	4
10,000-14,999	4	77	50	7	*
15,000 & over	2	77	35	9	*
Total − percent	100	61	29	69	15
− number	3,460	2,113	994	2,370	530

*denotes less than one-half of one percent

The pattern of mobility is apparent in the social security data (see Table 2.2). Whereas only 5 percent of the females earned $5,000 or more in 1962, 40 percent of the males earned more than $5,000. The higher earnings for males are explained by both the different occupational distributions between the sexes and the tendency for males to be assigned work more regularly. Even where males and females are found in the same job, men may have higher incomes because they work more often and are less affected by seasonal variations during the year. The percent of workers remaining in the industry, for both males and females, is about 60 percent, but in low income jobs males are far less likely to remain in the industry than females. At almost every income level, the males who remain are much more likely to advance. This is especially true at the levels between $3,000 and $6,000, where advancement to the more skilled positions is likely to take place.

Another way to examine the occupational structure of the garment industry is to ask how the better jobs are distributed. What percent of the higher wage positions are staffed through upgrading? Are the more desirable jobs equitably distributed among the races and sexes? Table 2.3 contains data which help to answer these questions.

About 30 percent of all jobs in the industry paid more than $4,000 in 1966; between 75 percent and 80 percent of these positions were filled by workers with at least four years experience in the industry. At these levels new entrants to the industry account for less than one job in four. In addition, most workers at these pay levels have been upgraded in the previous four years. That is, they had moved up at least one step in the income scale since 1962. Thus, while there are relatively few intermediate level jobs in the industry, those that do exist are filled largely with experienced and upgraded workers. Those who do move up constitute only a small fraction of the numerous low-wage workers and are disproportionately male and white. Females, who comprise over two-thirds of the total workforce, are severely underrepresented in higher wage jobs. Blacks are a much smaller proportion of the labor force, but they too are underrepresented in better jobs.

TRAINING AND OCCUPATIONAL MOBILITY

Training needs in the garment industry are minimal. Those entering the industry as operators, pressers, or shipping clerks are trained quickly and efficiently on the job. No training prior to entry is necessary, and the only job requirements are a degree of manual dexterity and good eyesight. Anyone with these attributes can acquire the requisite skills for any production job. The few higher level positions such as cutter or marker require no formal training; skills are acquired as a by-product of work at related lower level jobs.

Despite this pattern of informal on-the-job training there exists in New York City a vocational high school devoted to training for the garment industry. The High School of Fashion Industries (HSFI) has five different curricula intended to prepare youths for work in the garment industry. Approximately 2,000 students are enrolled in these courses at any one time.

The largest group of students are those preparing for work in the women's apparel segment of the industry. They include females in dressmaking and machine operating courses, as well as a smaller number of males enrolled in a women's garment manufacturing program. Graduates of these courses are qualified for positions as beginning operators along with other entrants to the industry. The program in men's clothing manufacturing is quite small, comprising fewer than 100 students, and is open only to males. There is both a technical and vocational fashion design program. Those in the technical program take sufficient academic work to qualify for college admission if they choose. Those in the vocational program are expected to enter the labor market immediately after graduation. Job openings for designers are very few in number and generally require years of experience in the industry, as well as college training. Most vocational students and many technical students are never employed as designers.

A recently completed study of the HSFI found that it serves neither its students nor the industry very well. As part of her research the author, Sally Hillsman, used Social Security data to trace the work history of 1,950 individuals graduating from the school between 1956 and 1963. Only 565, or less than 29 percent, of the graduates were employed in the manufacture of apparel and related products four to six months after graduation. Informal estimates by industry representatives for more recent years are that the figure may now be as low as 5 percent. A second important finding of Hillsman's study was that graduates working in the industry earned substantially less than those who found employment in other fields. After analyzing data similar to that contained in Table 2.4, she concludes: "We have shown that trade related placement does not necessarily translate vocational training into greater general economic well-being than does unrelated placement. Indeed, the reverse is true for most graduates."[3]

The Fashion Institute of Technology (FIT), a community college operated as part of the State University of New York, is frequently mentioned as a source of skilled manpower for the garment industry, but certain qualifications must be made. The school offers associate degrees in four fields—advertising, business, design, and industrial technology. Most of the graduates do not go directly to work for garment manufacturers. They are likely to be employed by retail stores, advertising agencies, or trade magazines. Only those students majoring in apparel design are likely to work for a manufacturer, and they usually begin as assistants to designers. FIT is primarily a source of white collar

[3] Sally T. Hillsman, *Entry into the Labor Market: The Preparation and Job Placement of Negro and White High School Graduates* (PhD dissertation, Columbia University, 1970), ch. vii, p. 25.

Table 2.4   Median Quarterly Earnings of HSFI Graduates Four to Six Months
after Graduation

Course and Race	Type of Employment	
	Trade Related	Unrelated
Fashion Design – Technical		
Negro & Puerto Rican	$372	$687
Other	608	655
Fashion Design – Vocational		
Negro	474	548
Puerto Rican	609	678
Other	658	680
Trade Dressmaking		
Negro	513	422
Puerto Rican	524	574
Other	591	661
Garment Operating		
Negro	433	441
Puerto Rican	498	296
Other	541	572

SOURCE: Hillsman, *Entry into the Labor Market*, Table VII-8

manpower (assistant buyer, copy writer, fashion illustrator) for retail stores and business services related only indirectly to what is traditionally called the garment industry.

Government training programs have not been used to prepare workers for the garment industry. The simplest explanation is that they have not been needed. Employers have traditionally trained new workers, who are frequently drawn from disadvantaged segments of the population. It is unnecessary for the government to subsidize this process. Undoubtedly other factors have been influential. The affected unions have pressured administrators to exclude the industry from MDTA benefits because they feared the program would be used to train new workers by "runaway shops" who flee existing supplies of labor in search of cheaper nonunion manpower.

EXPANDING UPGRADING OPPORTUNITIES

The most important factor limiting upgrading in the garment industry is the occupational structure of the industry. There are simply very few high wage jobs into which individuals can move. This situation

25

is likely to be altered only through change in the technology of the production process which increases productivity and shifts manpower requirements. Prospects for significant changes of this type are not good. The only automated techniques being developed are in the cutting and sizing processes. The limited quantities in which any single size and style are produced restrict the applicability of these and other automated procedures. The small plant size and rapid, unpredictable style changes also hamper the introduction of technological advances. At present there does not seem to be any projected change in the production process, although some automated cutting devices are likely to be adopted slowly. These will reduce the number of high wage, rather than low wage, positions.

In New York City some change in the occupational structure of the local industry is likely to result from the flight of many contract shops to lower wage regions of the nation and the increased reliance upon imports from foreign countries. These moves reduce the total employment and most affect machine operator and other low wage positions. At the same time the higher wage functions, such as design and sales, have remained and perhaps grown in importance in New York. This trend toward the geographic separation of functions within the overall manufacturing process has enabled the city to retain the better jobs while eliminating the less desirable ones.

There are few opportunities to increase the percentage of better paying jobs which are filled by the industry's internal labor supply. Nearly 80 percent of all jobs paying more than $5,000 are already filled with workers from the industry. Perhaps pressers, who receive relatively high wages, could be recruited from experienced machine operators as well as new entrants to the industry. But some women may still prefer to remain operators rather than work at the hot pressing machines. Raising the proportion of high wage jobs filled through upgrading above the present 80 percent level is not a very likely possibility. The upgrading that does take place in the industry depends on the informal acquisition of skills. Formal training is generally not related to upgrading.

While better jobs in the industry are typically reserved for experienced workers, not all workers are given equal access. Males are highly overrepresented in the group that advances, and many skilled jobs are reserved exclusively for males. There may be little opportunity to expand the *number* of individuals who move up the occupational ladder, but it is possible to insure that those who do advance are drawn fairly from the total population of lower level workers.

3

The Food Service Industry

OVERVIEW OF THE INDUSTRY

The food service industry does not conform neatly to the standard industrial classifications frequently used to categorize the economic functions of establishments. The majority of workers in the field are employed by retail eating and drinking places which are commonly referred to as restaurants and bars. Another sizeable group work in restaurants operated by hotels and motels. The industry also encompasses workers at restaurants or fountains operated by other retail stores, amusement centers, and cafeterias provided by commercial plants for their employees. Finally, there is a large group, estimated at over one-half million nationally, engaged in what is termed institutional feeding—that is, food service operations at large institutions such as schools, hospitals, and prisons.

Because it is distributed over such a wide variety of establishments and overlaps several functional categories, it is difficult to obtain precise figures on the size and nature of employment in the total industry in New York City. The 1970 average annual employment in retail eating and drinking places for the city was 119,100. The total annual average figure for hotels and motels was 30,000, of which approximately 30 percent were engaged in the preparation or serving of food and drink.[1] Based upon data gathered in an earlier study we can estimate that for every ten employees in retail eating and drinking places there is one employee in food service operations at other retail and manufacturing enterprises.[2] Therefore, about 12,000 workers in New York City are in food service occupations in businesses besides restaurants or hotels. This yields a subtotal of approximately 140,000 workers, exclusive of those in hospitals, schools, and other institutions. An educated guess, and there is little one can do except guess, of the total of food service industry employment in New York City would be 170,000.

Workers in the industry are likely to be employed in small establishments. About 35 percent of the employees in all retail eating and drinking places in New York State are in establishments with fewer than 10 employees, and about 40 percent are in businesses having 10 to 49 employees.[3] Most other food service operations are likely to fall within these size categories also, although they may be a part of much larger organizations. Since the school cafeteria worker is unlikely to move into an academic discipline and the drug store fountain man unlikely to be promoted to pharmacist, it is sensible to consider these small departments as separate entities in discussing job mobility and training.

There is little variation in the occupational structure of retail eating and drinking places and restaurants associated with other businesses. The most important differences are the greater proportion of counter waiters in other enterprises, reflecting the large number of counter facilities at drug stores and variety stores. Such establishments are also less likely to employ bartenders, since they rarely serve alchoholic beverages.

Because of the unconventional compensation system in the industry, survey data tend to underestimate the actual earnings of many workers. Data on median weekly and hourly cash wages in retail eating and

[1] *Employment Review* (May, 1971), Table 3, pp. 19-21.

[2] New York State Department of Labor, "Special Labor News Memorandum Number 123," May 15, 1969.

[3] Based on data from U.S. Bureau of the Census, *County Business Patterns, 1967, New York*, CBP-67-34 (Washington, D.C., 1968).

drinking places are presented in Table 3.1. It is important to note, however, that according to the same source 83 percent of the food service workers received some addition to their cash wages. Most (48 percent) received only one or two free meals, but many (32 percent) received both meals and tips; a few (3 percent) received only tips. Generally the value of meals is minimal; tips are more difficult to assess. Waiters and waitresses are frequently the only tipped employees, al-

Table 3.1 Wages of Nonexempt Workers in Eating and Drinking Places in New York City, March, 1966

Occupation	Number Workers	Median Hourly Wage	Median Weekly Wages
All occupations	113,871	$1.62	$61.46
Workers receiving no addition to wage	13,593	1.89	67.91
Workers receiving meals and/or tips	100,278	1.59	60.50
Table waiter	23,820	1.10	34.72
Counter waiter	10,098	1.43	54.92
Busboy	4,483	1.39	50.41
Bartender	10,502	1.99	79.73
Cafeteria counter-man	2,683	1.72	66.51
General cafeteria worker	2,365	1.49	56.15
Cook, chef, baker	11,855	2.36	99.08
Dishwasher	8,160	1.54	63.44
Other kitchen title	12,579	1.84	73.99
Porter	4,154	1.56	62.07
Other restaurant title	4,187	1.91	72.10
Cashier	2,043	1.84	65.40
Other clerical	801	2.30	90.06
Salesclerk	402	1.76	67.68
Delivery boy	1,098	.93	25.71
Other	1,048	1.74	61.59

SOURCE: New York State Department of Labor, Special Labor News Memorandum Number 123, May 15, 1969.

though bartenders also receive some additional income this way. There are no accurate data on this source of income, in part because workers tend to minimize the figure when dealing with the Internal Revenue Service and maximize it for the computation of Social Security contributions and benefits. While there is likely to be substantial variation in tips among types of establishments, one can estimate that most waiters and waitresses earn in tips at least as much and some cases more than double their regular hourly wages.

The data in Table 3.1 include only employees covered by the minimum wage provisions of New York State law and thus exclude certain managerial and administrative personnel. From 1960 census data it can be estimated that about 15 percent of the total work force fell into this category, a figure inflated by the fact that all establishments have managers and proprietors and the industry is characterized by a large number of small establishments.[4] In many smaller units the proprietor may also fill the role of cook and bottle-washer.

According to a survey of eating and drinking places in metropolitan areas of the Northeast United States, about 45 percent of the industry's workers are female. About two-thirds of the women are waitresses, an occupation which is dominated by females. Less than 20 percent of the waiters and waitresses were male. Women are a relatively small percentage of most other major occupational groups, comprising, for example, less than 10 percent of all bartenders and dishwashers.[5]

OCCUPATIONAL MOBILITY

Entry into and mobility within the industry can best be discussed in terms of three broad and sometimes overlapping categories of personnel—kitchen, dining room, and managerial. The largest group are those performing dining room or serving functions—waiters, busboys, cafeteria countermen, etc. Almost all of these positions can be described as ports of entry; they are open to those entering the industry

[4]U.S. Bureau of the Census, *U.S. Census of Population: 1960, Subject Reports, Occupational By Industry*, Final Report PC (2)-7C (Washington, D.C., 1963), Table 2.

[5]Bureau of Labor Statistics, *Industry Wage Survey—Eating and Drinking Places*, Bulletin 1588, April, 1968.

and those entering the labor force. Educational requirements range from none to minimal. Waiters may have to read a menu and add a check, but cafeteria workers or busboys do not even perform these tasks. Some luxury restaurants may hire only experienced help, but it is not essential. Witness the way in which large numbers of students are trained literally overnight for work as waiters in luxurious resort hotels each summer. In almost every case new employees receive whatever brief training is needed from the firm.

There is little occupational mobility within the dining room. Occasionally a busboy may be promoted to waiter. Probably more important is inter-firm mobility within the same broad occupational group. Waiters increase their earnings by gaining experience and contacts and by moving into openings at higher priced restaurants where the tips are likely to be greater. For dining room workers increased earnings often come from employer shifts without occupational changes.

Kitchen and food preparation employees are the second largest group. Porters and dishwashers are paid low hourly wages and in some establishments receive a free meal. The jobs require no special skills and almost anyone can be taught in a very short time to do the job. The category "other kitchen worker" includes individuals doing a variety of tasks including cleaning, receiving supplies, cutting and otherwise preparing food for cooking, and assisting cooks or bakers in their work. These jobs are open to inexperienced workers who learn by informal observation and instruction in the kitchen. The exact combination of tasks a helper performs will vary with his desire to learn, the workload placed upon the cook, and the willingness of the cook to teach. By watching and listening the helper may pick up the skills which may enable him to move into a cook's position. Frequently this involves several job changes in order to find firms and cooks who provide the opportunity to learn new skills. Piore and Taylor described the process as follows:

The first and most fundamental characteristic of cook training is that it is worker programmed. The individual can program his own on-the-job training through frequent job changes, remaining in one establishment so long as he has something to learn there, moving on when the job is no longer instructive. Sometimes the movement is vertical, involving heavier responsibility, more skill, or better pay and/or working conditions. But lateral moves, motivated solely by the exhaustion of learning opportunities or the search for higher quality instruction, are also frequent. These worker-initiated job changes generate the kind of exposure to tasks and skills provided elsewhere by movement along an internal line of progression or supervised rotation of work assignments. The training on the job is supplemented by formal institutional instruction in the culinary arts (e.g., baking, haute cuisine, meat cutting, tallow carving, and the like) obtained, for the most part, from specialized proprietary schools. The courses are not standard; the trainee must piece together his curriculum from a variety of different schools. Some of the chefs interviewed for this study appeared to have attended classes intermittently over ten or fifteen year periods.[6]

Many cooks have acquired their skills in this way. Others have received formal training in European countries, but immigration restrictions have severely limited this source of manpower. Some formal instruction is available in the large cities of the United States, but today many of the cooks and bakers who have some formal training received it in the Armed Forces. This combination of unstructured learning and occasional formal instruction is the way individuals become cooks.

Bartenders both prepare and serve drinks and frequently function as their own cashier. The skills required are often overestimated and most bartenders learn their craft quickly. As a study of hotel employment has noted, "the typical bartender can learn to mix 95 percent of the drinks he will be called upon to make in an eight hour shift in a matter of hours, despite the aesthetic belief that it takes 15 years to learn how to mix a good dry martini."[7] As with waiters there is generally no occupational mobility and earnings are increased by performing the same job at higher priced establishments.

Most managerial personnel in restaurants are owners of their businesses. According to the 1960 census more than three of every four managers in the industry were self-employed. Salaried officials are

---

[6] David Taylor and Michael Piore, "Federal Training Programs for Dispersed Employment Occupations" (Massachusetts Institute of Technology, Department of Economics, Working Paper Number 42, December, 1968), p. 8.

[7] John Henderson, *Labor Market Institutions and Wages in the Lodging Industry* (East Lansing: Michigan State University, 1965), p. 155.

usually found only in larger businesses, chain organizations, and restaurants operated as a part of other businesses. Employers of salaried managers seek individuals with college degrees or, at a minimum, some post-high school educational experience. College graduates in business administration or in special programs in hotel and restaurant management are sought by the industry. Because this industry typically pays less than others and because it has a less glamorous image, these potential managers have been difficult to recruit. Consequently junior college graduates and those with some college experience have been hired as assistant managers or management trainees. Enrollment in college level hotel and restaurant management programs is growing and it is estimated that graduates from these programs numbered over 1,100 in 1971 compared with only 622 in 1966.[8] Despite this rapid growth the number of graduates is relatively low and they account for only a small proportion of restaurant managers. Most salaried management personnel are former owners. There is a high rate of business failure in eating and drinking establishments, which produces a high turnover of proprietors. Many cooks, waiters, or others with pantry (supply) experience eventually open their own businesses, often unsuccessfully. The National Restaurant Association estimated that in 1966 fewer than half the nation's restaurants were operated by the same owner for five years or more.[9] The former owners constitute a large pool of available management personnel for organizations seeking salaried officials.

The Social Security data (Table 3.2) reflect the high turnover and limited promotional opportunity which characterize the industry. Less than half the 1962 workforce was still working in the industry in 1966 and only slightly more than one-third of those remaining experienced a wage gain averaging $1,000. Most individuals working in the industry are employed at low wage levels and either remain at those levels or leave the industry.

The figures in Table 3.3 illustrate some important points about the structure of the food service industry's internal labor market. Over

[8]National Restaurant Association, "The Status of Food Service Education in the United States, 1970" (Chicago: National Restaurant Association, 1970).

[9]National Restaurant Association, "Facts About the Food Service Industry, 1970" (Chicago: National Restaurant Association, 1970).

Table 3.2   The 1966 Status of Workers in Eating and Drinking Places in New
York City in 1962 by Their 1962 Income

1962 Income	Percent of Total	Percent in Industry in 1966	Percent of Stayers Moving Up
$1-999	27%	23%	46%
1,000-1,999	21	52	27
2,000-2,999	18	52	40
3,000-3,999	15	63	35
4,000-4,999	9	61	43
5,000-5,999	5	69	34
6,000-6,999	3	73	47
7,000-7,999	1	63	10
8,000-8,999	1	56	80
9,000-9,999	*	33	*
10,000-14,999	1	57	25
15,000 & over	1	89	*
Total − percent	100	48	36
− number	1,574	757	275

*denotes less than one-half of one percent

Table 3.3   Characteristics of Workers in Eating and Drinking Places in New York
City in 1966 by Their 1966 Income

1966 Income	Percent of Total	Percent in Industry in 1962	Percent Upgraded since 1962	Percent Female	Percent Negro
$1-999	32%	36%	*	46%	19%
1,000-1,999	19	48	9%	37	16
2,000-2,999	13	56	19	17	22
3,000-3,999	13	55	29	23	20
4,000-4,999	9	59	36	12	15
5,000-5,999	6	74	50	6	19
6,000-6,999	4	72	49	17	8
7,000-7,999	2	82	70	4	15
8,000-8,999	1	50	50	17	17
9,000-9,999	1	80	60	40	*
10,000-14,999	1	87	67	13	*
15,000 & over	1	100	38	*	*
Total − percent	100	51	19	29	18
− number	1,402	715	267	412	245

* denotes less than one-half of one percent

35

three-fourths of the jobs pay less than $4,000. These are generally entry jobs, filled by new entrants. Upgrading plays only a small part in staffing. In contrast, the relatively small number of higher wage positions have few new entrants and are generally reserved for experienced workers; recent upgrading accounts for more than half the incumbents in positions of $5,000 and above.

Women are disporportionately represented in the lowest levels of the income scale. To a large degree this is explained by their concentration in waitress positions, which frequently are part-time and low-wage jobs. There is little prospect for increased earnings because most high priced restaurants use waiters rather than waitresses and because females are usually not recruited or promoted to the kitchen or management positions that provide higher salaries. Consequently, few women are able to move into better paying jobs. Negroes are proportionately represented in almost all categories but the highest paying jobs. These positions are primarily managerial, so it appears that blacks have an opportunity to move into all kitchen and dining room jobs, but are not hired as managers or supervisors.

TRAINING AND OCCUPATIONAL MOBILITY

For most workers in the food service industry training is an informal process which takes place on the job. Employers are responsible for providing whatever minimal training is needed for about 80 percent of the industry's labor force.

New York City has a vocational high school, the Food and Maritime Trades High School, devoted to training for the industry. Enrollment in the school has declined almost 50 percent over the past decade and is now about 400. School officials attribute this to the industry's poor image, compared to the many more glamorous growth industries in the city. Drop-out rates are high (about 60 percent) and in 1969 only 59 students graduated. Of this total, the school reports that 27 went on to employment in the industry, at wages averaging between $1.95 and $2.00 per hour. An almost equal number (23) continued school full-time, most of them at a community college program in hotel and restaurant management. The remainder were either employed in some other industry or were unemployed. Given the high percentage of graduates going on to college and the relatively low wages paid to graduates who accept training related jobs, it appears that the most important function of this institution is to enable a small number of students who might otherwise have dropped out to endure their high school experience and to continue in the educational system. Those who leave the system after graduation are usually hired only for kitchen helper or cook's assistant positions, which are open to almost any high school graduate and those with even less education.

The evening program operated by the Food and Maritime Trades High School is of greater significance to the industry. Courses lasting an average of eleven weeks are offered during the year and registration is open only to those employed in the industry. Course content is determined by industry need and students are frequently referred by their employers. In contrast to the day program, enrollment in these courses is growing: over 300 students are now participating in the various courses and sessions offered each year.

The training available locally in the private sector is of little importance for those seeking job mobility. Craig Claiborne of the New York *Times* reviews cooking schools in New York City annually. His most recent column listed nineteen schools open to all kinds of students.[10] While one or two small schools specializing in party and catering techniques were reasonably priced and might benefit those who earned their living in the field, the others averaged $20 to $35 per lesson and were likely to draw their students from housewives and amateur chefs who preferred to consume rather than market the fruits of their labor. Several curricula centered around full-course meals prepared and enjoyed by the class.

The Culinary Arts Institute in New Haven is a well-known school for chefs which offers a full-time, two-year program for approximately 1,000 students.[11] Total costs including tuition, room, board, and supplies exceed $5,000. Graduates are recognized as well-qualified chefs and generally are able to find employment at better restaurants or

---

[10] Craig Claiborne, "Cooking Classes Should Please Armchair Travelers," New York *Times*, September 8, 1970, p. 48.

[11] Craig Claiborne, "School Where Chefs are Made," New York *Times*, January 28, 1971, p. 41.

hotels. This is the only institutional training available which permits a recent high school graduate to qualify for higher level kitchen positions without working for some time in the industry, and each year a few graduates from New York City schools enroll at the institute.

New York City Community College has a two-year associate degree program in hotel and restaurant administration. Graduates are able to move into positions as supervisors and assistant managers at larger establishments. The program has been growing and enrollment is now over 200 students. Many colleges in New York City have programs in business administration, but no institution in the city has a baccalaureate program specifically designed for hotel or restaurant administration. There are 19 institutions nationally offering such programs with a total annual output of over 800 graduates.

In New York City training has been provided under federal programs for food service occupations. The Manpower Development Training program sponsored by the Board of Education offered two classes in food preparation in 1967-68. A total of 165 individuals enrolled, of which 100 completed the training. There are no data on the nature of the placements and level of earnings for the trainees, so it is not known if they moved into the industry or at what levels.

The Culinary Arts Development Program sponsored by Local 89 of the Chefs, Cooks, Pastry Cooks, and Assistants Union has been operating with funds provided under the MDTA for the last four years. The training is open to current restaurant employees. They receive their regular wages and attend training for one day per week for 26 weeks. Employers are reimbursed up to $20 per day for the wages paid workers while they are in training. Classes usually have a capacity of about 100 and are filled at the beginning of each course, although this requires some recruitment effort on the part of the union sponsors. Typically, 85 to 90 percent of the enrollees finish the program. Upon completion of the course workers are either promoted by their current employers or the union assists them in finding advanced positions at restaurants which have openings.

EXPANDING UPGRADING OPPORTUNITIES

Occupational mobility in the food service industry is dependent upon a variety of factors; training has only secondary importance. First, the occupational distribution of jobs in the industry shows the vast majority to be of an unskilled nature. Excluding supervisory workers, only one job in nine falls into the category of cook, chef, or baker and requires some special preparation. In the dining room there are no jobs which require formal training and there is no significant occupational mobility. One increases earnings by moving to higher priced establishments in order to earn larger tips, a process which requires ambition and personal contacts but is unrelated to the acquisition of new skills. It is primarily in the kitchen or food preparation job cluster that some potential for occupational mobility exists.

Even if one looks at the kitchen as a distinct department with its own internal labor market, there is still an unfavorable ratio of skilled to unskilled jobs. There are two unskilled workers in the kitchen for every cook, chef, or baker. This ratio is likely to increase in the future because of the technological and marketing factors now reshaping the industry. Increased utilization of frozen and ready-to-serve foods and prepared mixes and sauces, as well as the tendency for restaurants to specialize and thus reduce the variety of items on their menus, will result in a need for fewer and less skilled employees for food preparation.

Despite this unfavorable long-run outlook, it does appear that expanded training opportunities for kitchen helpers could facilitate their occupational mobility. The methods currently used to train cooks do not produce a satisfactory number of adequately prepared candidates. The pattern of informal training, observation, and worker programmed instruction contributes to the high turnover and low productivity which characterize the industry. Public sponsorship of training for those employed in the industry is serving to help meet the needs of employers and employees. The evening program at the Food and Maritime Trades High School and the training sponsored by Local 89 are steps in this direction. Continuation and selected expansion of these and similar efforts should be encouraged. This type of training is one way in which government intervention might be of assistance in helping individuals achieve occupational mobility.

For management personnel training is important, but there is less need to expand federal efforts. The positions usually require post-high school training, and in New York the rapidly expanding community college system is responding to the needs. The graduates produced there and in other colleges, combined with the present surplus of former owners of small restaurants, are likely to constitute an adequate supply. Some part-time training opportunities in the field might enable some of those employed at lower levels in the industry to advance to supervisory positions.

The food service industry is undergoing organizational changes which may affect the nature of its internal labor market. An increasing percentage of the industry is taking the form of franchise or chain operations. There are no accurate data relating to this phenomenon on a local basis and the national figures are misleading. The Department of Commerce reported that in 1969 retail eating and drinking places in the United States had total sales of approximately $25,854 million of which $2,477 million was accounted for by chain stores.[12] But its definition of "chain store" does not include franchise operations and only includes those chains having at least eleven units. The National Franchise Association reported that there are 236 organizations with about 30,000 units franchisizing food service operations, so the proportions of total industry sales represented by chain and franchise operations is undoubtedly far greater than the 9.6 percent which the Commerce Department figures indicate. A better estimate is more than double that figure, or about 20 percent, with continued increases expected in the future.

Chain and franchise operations are experiencing rapid growth because their standardized purchasing and preparation have made possible greater productivity than that of independent businesses. Because productivity, indicated by sales per employee, is high, the proportion of employment represented by this segment of the industry is less than their share of the sales. But the impact of chain and franchise operations is still significant, probably about 15 percent of the total food service employment in New York. An important consequence of this trend is that somewhat higher wage rates are made possible by the improved productivity. Second, the growth of these firms may improve

[12] U.S. Department of Commerce, *U.S. Industrial Outlook, 1970* (Washington, D.C., 1970, pp. 410-11.

prospects for occupational mobility because they often provide training at central locations for key personnel and provide unit operators with manuals and other materials for training employees at the individual stores.

A model for career progression in the food service industry has been developed by a research group at the Cornell University School of Hotel Administration.[13] Several points should be made about the likelihood of its widespread and successful implementation. First, it includes a wide variety of occupational titles and specialties which are found only in the largest enterprises. Most food service employment is in smaller firms or units where one individual performs several functions. Second, the higher level positions are far smaller in number than those at the bottom, so that promotional opportunities occur infrequently. Most advancement is likely to continue to take place as a result of employer shifts rather than promotions. Finally, internal movement into managerial positions is likely to be blocked by educational requirements associated with these jobs, although part-time training could eliminate this obstacle.

The food service industry does offer a limited potential for increased occupational mobility through expansion of training opportunities; however, given the large and increasing ratio of unskilled to skilled positions and the relatively low wage scale which prevails in the industry, one must be cautious in appraising the significance of this potential.

[13] School of Hotel Administration, Cornell University, *A Study of Career Ladders and Manpower Development for Nonmanagement Personnel in the Food Industry* (Cornell University, 1970).

41

4

Health Services

OVERVIEW OF THE INDUSTRY

Health services is a booming industry. Nationally, total expenditures for health services rose from less than $27 billion in 1960 to a figure likely to have exceeded $70 billion in 1970. Employment in the industry has practically doubled in the past ten years, growing from 1,454,000 in 1959 to 2,856,000 in 1969. This expanding industry provides a wide variety of job opportunities for New Yorkers. While there are no precise figures, one can estimate that over 200,000 individuals are presently engaged in the provision of health services in New York City.

These workers are employed in a variety of settings. A large majority, probably close to 70 percent, are employed in the 140 hospitals located in the five boroughs.[1] The remainder are distributed among numerous nursing homes, private offices, clinics, laboratories, and other related institutions. Because it accounts for such a large percentage of the labor force and because very few occupations found in the industry are not represented, the hospital is the most reasonable focus for a discussion of training and job mobility in the industry.

[1] On employing firms, see, Harry Greenfield and Carol Brown. *Allied Health Manpower: Trends and Prospects* (New York: Columbia University Press, 1969) pp. 98–104.

42

HEALTH SERVICES

There are a number of available sources from which one can derive a picture of the occupational structure of employment in the city's hospitals.[2] Despite their individual limitations and differences these studies all present a similar picture of the hospital occupational structure. First, there is an enormous variety of occupations found within the hospital. A research group at the City University of New York reported 232 active job titles in municipal hospitals. Table 4.1 is adapted from that study and provides information for all titles having at least 100 employees. The 36 job titles represent 33,082 out of a total of 35,900 employees.

Table 4.1 Employment in New York City Municipal Hospitals

Occupation	Number of Employees[a]	Percent of Total	Wage Level[b]	Staffing Condition
Medical Care	*2,189*	*6.1%*		
Intern	289	.8	$4,850–6,290	Adequate
Resident	918	2.6	6,400–8,200	Adequate
Physician	982	2.7	NA	Adequate
Nursing Care	*15,667*	*43.7%*		
Nurse aide	8,039	22.4	4,550–5,990	Adequate
Pupil LPN	131	.4	–	NA
Practical nurse	2,731	7.6	5,150–6,590	Adequate
Pupil RN	1,423	4.0	–	NA
Staff nurse	1,418	3.9	8,200–10,300	Chronic, Critical
Head nurse	1,078	3.0	9,400–11,500	Chronic, Critical
Supervisor, nurses	681	1.9	12,100–14,500	Chronic, Critical
Ass't superintendant, nurses	166	.5	NA	Adequate

[2] National data are available in U.S. Bureau of the Census, *U.S. Census of Population, 1960*, Subject Reports, Occupation by Industry, Final Report PC (2) -7C (Washington, D.C., 1960); New York State data are found in New York State Department of Labor, *Manpower Needs in Health Services* (Albany; N.Y.S. Dept. of Labor, 1969), and New York State Department of Health, *Hospital Manpower Survey, 1969* (Albany: N.Y.S. Dept. of Health, 1970); New York City data are available in reports prepared annually by the United Hospital Fund specifying employment by hospital department and in wage surveys conducted by the Bureau of Labor Statistics in 1960, 1963, 1966, 1969, and 1970; data relating to New York City municipal hospitals are found in Eleanor Gilpatrick and Paul Corliss, *The Occupational Structure of New York City Municipal Hospitals* (New York: Health Services Mobility Study, Research Report Number 2, 1969).

43

Table 4.1 Continued

Occupation	Number of Employees[a]	Percent of Total	Wage Level[b]	Staffing Condition
Food Service	*3,211*	*8.7%*		
Dietary aide	2,588	7.2	4,550–5,990	Adequate
Cook	337	.9	7,100–8,900	Adequate
Dietician	178	.5	7,100–8,900	Serious shortage
Head dietician	108	.1	9,400–11,500	Serious shortage
Other Health Related	*6,361*	*17.8%*		
Institutional aide	2,326	6.5	4,550–5,990	Adequate
Housekeeping aide	2,292	6.4	4,550–5,990	Adequate
Laboratory aide	247	.7	5,150–6,590	High turnover
X-ray technician	199	.6	5,750–7,190	Chronic, Critical
Occupational therapy	606	1.7	8,200–10,300	Chronic, Critical
Social worker	174	.5	9,850–12,250	Chronic, Critical
Hospital clerk	517	1.4	4,250–5,330	Adequate
Other Listed Titles	*5,654*	*15.9%*		
Clerk	1,578	4.4	4,850–6,290	High turnover
Messenger	422	1.2	4,850–6,290	Adequate
Typist	398	1.1	4,850–6,290	High turnover
Stenographer	345	1.0	5,150–6,590	Serious shortage
Telephone operator	168	.5	5,150–6,590	Adequate
Senior clerk	260	.7	6,400–8,200	Adequate
Supervisory clerk	117	.3	8,600–10,700	Adequate
Laundry worker	444	1.2	4,000–5,080	High turnover
Senior laundry worker	272	.8	4,250–5,330	High turnover
Elevator operator	529	1.5	4,550–5,990	Adequate
Motor vehicle oper.	504	1.4	6,750–8,550	Adequate
Maintenance man	307	.9	7,800–9,600	Adequate
Stationary engineer	100	.3	10,750–13,150	Serious shortage
Special officer	210	.6	4,550–5,990	Adequate
Total – listed titles	*33,082*	*92.2%*		
Total – all titles	*35,900*	*100.0%*		

[a]–Full-time equivalent as of February, 1967.

[b]–Approximate annual wages as of May, 1968.

SOURCE: Eleanor Gilpatrick and Paul Corliss, *The Occupational Structure of New York City Municipal Hospitals* (New York: Health Services Mobility Study, Research Report Number 2, 1969), vol. 1, ch. 3, p. 3.

Second, there is a wide range of education and training requirements for these jobs. Educational requirements range from none to the more than twenty years of training required for medical specialists. The majority of hospital employees are required to have little or no formal training to obtain their jobs. As Table 4.2 indicates, for those jobs for which information was available, over 11,500 workers had to meet no special entry requirements, and another 11,500 needed only 8 to 9 years of schooling. A total of 68.5 percent of the filled hospital jobs did not require a full high school education. Of the remaining jobs 8 percent required only a high school diploma, about 10 percent an associate degree, 5 percent a bachelor's degree, 1 percent a master's, and 8 percent a more advanced degree.

Table 4.2 Educational Requirements for Municipal Hospital Jobs

Years of School Required[a]	Number of Job Titles[b]	Employment	
		Number	Percent
No special requirements	49	11,583	34.4%
8 to 9 years	16	11,482	34.1
High school diploma	25	2,700	8.0
14 years or Associate	8	3,253	9.7
15 to 16 or Baccalaureate	53	1,783	5.3
17 to 18 or Masters	13	352	1.0
20 years or Doctorate	28	2,521	7.5
Total	192	33,674	100.0

[a]—Exclusive of trade-off for experience.
[b]—Data not available for all job titles.

SOURCE: Eleanor Gilpatrick and Paul Corliss, *The Occupational Structure of New York City Municipal Hospitals* (New York: Health Services Mobility Study, Research Report Number 2, 1969), ch. 2, p. 3, vol. 1.

The next important point to note is that perceived shortages exist primarily in job titles requiring an associate degree or above. The five major aide titles, which require no special training, as well as numerous other job titles requiring only basic skills (clerk, messenger, maintenance man) are all judged to be adequately staffed. Chronic and critical shortages were reported to exist among professional nurses, occupational therapists, X-ray technicians, and social workers—all technical and professional positions.

Finally, most hospital employees are female, but women are not found in uniformly high percentages in all occupations. National census figures reported that almost 70 percent of health workers were female, while the same figure for workers in all industries was only about one-third. But female participation in the industry varied among occupations from a low of under 10 percent for staff physicians to a high of well over 90 percent in many nursing department positions. In general women tended to be concentrated in lower level positions and were not well represented in the more prestigious and better paid occupations.

OCCUPATIONAL MOBILITY

Occupational mobility in the hospital generally takes place within the several independent departments which comprise the institution. Each department consists of several occupational titles which reflect the unit's unique function. Mobility is generally restricted to the department.

The primary responsibility for the direct provision of medical care rests with the interns, residents, and staff physicians. According to the municipal system data, they account for about 6 percent of all hospital employment. For all hospitals in the city the figure was close to 9 percent. Hospitals draw their interns from a national pool of graduating medical students and their residents primarily from a national pool of graduating interns; some practicing physicians take a resident position in order to qualify as certified specialists. Hospital staff positions are filled by those who have recently completed residencies and by the specialists throughout the nation already in private practice. Perhaps more than any other occupation these medical practitioners work in a truly national labor market. Husband hunters as well as manpower experts have long recognized that anyone completing medical school will have a sizeable income and almost unlimited job opportunities.

For those engaged in nursing services, a group representing over 40 percent of all hospital employees, the opportunity structure is very different. Aide positions require no special skills or training. An aide is paid about $100 per week and generally remains an aide, for there are no direct promotion opportunities. Licensed practical nurses (LPN) must have a minimum of eight years of education and one academic year of specialized training in a state-approved program before they are eligible to take the licensing exam. While receiving somewhat higher pay than an aide, the LPN also has no direct promotional opportunities. Registered nurses (RN) or staff nurses must complete a minimum of two years of specialized post-high-school training in an approved program before they can take the state licensing exam. An RN does have some potential career mobility. After working as a staff nurse for a year she is likely to be eligible for a position as a head nurse and eventually as a nurse supervisor. A registered nurse beginning in a staff nurse position at $8,200 might eventually move up to a supervisory post paying a maximum of $14,500 per year.

The medical laboratory and X-ray departments each have their own occupational divisions. Personnel in both departments are licensed, the former by the City of New York and the latter by the state. Anyone, other than a doctor or dentist, operating X-ray equipment must complete a special two-year, post-high-school training program approved by the New York State Department of Health. Employed X-ray technicians earn a moderate salary and some may receive salary increments or be promoted to senior positions, but X-ray personnel work under a radiologist who has professional medical training. Employment in these occupations is about 1 percent of all hospital employment. According to the most recent BLS survey (1970), X-ray technicians averaged $159 per week and chief X-ray technicians received an average of $211 per week.[3]

Employed in the medical laboratory are lab assistants, technicians, technologists, and pathologists, who together comprise less than 5 percent of all hospital workers. Assistants are usually required to have a high school diploma but need not have any other special training. Technicians must either have completed a two-year training program approved by the city or pass an examination given by the city. Assistants may qualify as technicians by taking the exam, but job experience alone is usually not enough; some formal classroom instruction is al-

---

[3] These and other average salary figures are from Bureau of Labor Statistics, "Earnings of Hospital Workers in New York City, April, 1970," Industry Wage Survey Report 71-1, February, 1971.

most always needed to pass the more academic portions of the exam. A technologist position requires either a bachelor degree in some scientific discipline or completion of a special four-year program. The pathologist is a physician with specialist training. Salaries range from approximately $110 per week for a laboratory aide to an average of $165 per week for medical technologists.

In addition to the departmental tasks outlined above, each hospital usually employs several varieties of allied health professionals who perform unique functions. Included in this group are occupational therapists, physical therapists, pharmacists, and social workers. Each of these occupations has its own special pre-employment requirements which include at least a baccalaureate degree and frequently completion of a special graduate program. Individuals may be promoted to a limited number of senior or supervisory positions in their specific field. Typical salaries in these occupations are $192.50 per week for social workers and $175 per week for physical therapists. Total employment in these professions is about 5 percent of all hospital employment.

Hospitals must feed their patients as well as provide them with medical treatment, and the food service department accounts for about one of every ten hospital employees. At the bottom of the occupational structure are the numerous dietary aides. These positions have no special entry requirements. Receiving somewhat higher salaries are food-service supervisors who usually must have a high school diploma and some specialized training or related experience. Dieticians are required to have at least a bachelor degree in home economics or some related field. They may be promoted to supervisory positions as head dieticians. Salaries in the department range from approximately $110 weekly for aides to $155 for food-service supervisors and $162.50 for dieticians. The remaining hospital occupations and departments are not industry specific and will be given less attention. They include a large office and clerical segment and sizeable housekeeping and maintenance departments.

What emerges from this outline of the occupational structure of hospitals is an industry with numerous distinct internal labor markets. Horizontal mobility is practically non-existent. A lab technician cannot become an X-ray technician; a food-service supervisor cannot become a nursing supervisor. Vertical mobility is similarly limited by formal job requirements set by professional organizations and enforced by state and local licensing statutes, as well as by hospital accreditation procedures. From the available data it can be estimated that approximately 25 percent of all hospital employment in New York City is in categories requiring a license from one or more government agencies and that an additional 3 percent to 5 percent are in occupations which are not licensed but do have formal entry requirements set by professional associations and sometimes enforced through institutional accreditation standards. Nurse aides cannot become nurses without leaving their jobs to attend school; lab technicians also have to attend school to become technologists. The hospital occupational structure can hardly be described as a ladder; rather, it resembles a group of individual rungs randomly scattered up and down a very high wall.

The Social Security data (Table 4.3) indicate high rates of retention in the industry and a great deal of upward mobility in earnings. About two-thirds of all 1962 workers were working in the industry in 1966 and in most income categories the figure was substantially higher. In addition, nearly three-quarters of the workers remaining in the industry moved up the income scale at least one step, indicating a high rate of occupational mobility. It is likely that many of the gains in income level result from the general rise in hospital wages rather than a high incidence of occupational mobility. No precise figures are available for hospital wages in 1962 and 1966, but over this period as well as the remainder of the decade wages in the industry rose rapidly. For example, between 1960 and 1966 average weekly earnings of factory production workers in New York City rose 20.7 percent from $84.98 to $102.60 or $916 annually. For the same period average weekly wages for staff nurses rose 47.3 percent from $82.50 to $121.50 or $2,028 annually. For nurse aides the increase was 36.5 percent, from $57.50 to $78.50 or $1,092 annually; and for X-ray techicians it was 40.8 percent, from $78.50 to $110.50 or $1,664 annually.[4] These rapid and significant increases probably explain much of the income

[4] Bureau of Labor Statistics, "Recent Trends in Wages and Related Benefits of Hospital Workers in New York City," Regional Labor Statistics Bulletin Number 20, May, 1970.

Table 4.3   The 1966 Status of Workers in the Health Service Industry in 1962
            By Their 1962 Income

1962 Income	Percent of Total	Percent in Industry in 1966	Percent of Stayers Earning $1,000 More in 1966[a]	Percent of Stayers Earning $2,000 More in 1966[b]
$1-999	14%	29%	66%	49%
1,000-1,999	12	44	70	51
2,000-2,999	12	60	71	36
3,000-3,999	15	70	75	29
4,000-4,999	13	77	65	22
5,000-5,999	8	81	80	55
6,000-6,999	10	87	87	76
7,000-7,999	9	91	95	25
8,000-8,999	3	87	47	43
9,000-9,999	1	77	50	50
10,000-14,999	2	69	27	27
15,000 & over	1	64	*	*
Total − percent	100	66	74	40
− number	2,265	1,499	1,105	606

[a]—refers to those moving up one step on the income scale.
[b]—refers to those moving up two steps on the income scale, except those earning $9,000 and above.
*—denotes less than one-half of one percent

mobility recorded in the Social Security data. If we examine gains averaging $2,000, which are more likely to indicate occupational shifts, the figures are significantly reduced. Nonetheless, even if allowance is made for the wage gains, there exists a notable rate of occupational mobility. Over 40 percent of those remaining in the industry moved up an average of $2,000. This suggests that despite the narrowly defined internal labor markets and the obstacles of licensing requirements, many workers do manage to advance.

Data on the characteristics of health service workers in 1966 (Table 4.4) indicate that most of those at the lower levels (less than $4,000) are new entrants. Jobs paying between $4,000 and $7,999 are most often filled by experienced workers, with new entrants typically accounting for less than one third of the group. However, upgrading is relatively infrequent in these categories and we may estimate that

50

Table 4.4 Characteristics of Workers in the Health Services Industry in 1966 by Their 1966 Income

1966 Income	Percent of Total	Percent in Industry in 1962	Percent Upgraded since 1962[a]	Percent Female	Percent Negro
$1-999	11%	24%	*	66%	35%
1,000-1,999	8	35	*	68	30
2,000-2,999	8	38	6%	71	33
3,000-3,999	12	43	11	72	45
4,000-4,999	14	66	17	63	43
5,000-5,999	9	78	30	71	48
6,000-6,999	7	65	34	54	22
7,000-7,999	8	69	37	28	9
8,000-8,999	13	81	42	13	7
9,000-9,999	5	80	79	17	10
10,000-14,999	4	81	48	15	7
15,000 & over	2	67	56	2	8
Total – percent	100	59	24	51	29
– number	2,499	1,467	607	1,270	714

[a]–refers to those employed in the industry and earning an average of $2,000 less in 1962.

*–denotes less than one-half of one percent

intra-industry occupational mobility plays a less important role than the attraction of new workers to the industry in the staffing of these positions. About eight of ten jobs in the $8,000 to $14,999 categories are filled by experienced personnel and nearly half of them are likely to have been upgraded. Examples of such advancement include movement from staff nurse and technician to appropriate supervisory positions. It is in this range that upgrading appears to be most important, although it is possible that the data are inflated by wage gains within occupations that took place during this time and that exceed the estimates upon which the tables were based. At the highest level, which is likely to consist almost exclusively of physicians, new entry is more important. This is best explained by the transfer of physicians to salaried hospital employment from private practice, income from which is not recorded under the social security system. The high incidence of upgrading for experienced workers at this level may reflect the movement of residents into attending staff positions.

51

The Social Security data also re-emphasize the point that a heavy reliance on upgrading does not necessarily yield an even balance of jobs among the races. Upgrading is an important source of manpower for the approximately 20 percent of all jobs paying between $8,000 and $14,999. However, it is precisely in these categories where females and Negroes are most seriously underrepresented as a percentage of the workforce. Many of the better jobs may be reserved for workers at the lower levels, but it is not always true that all workers have equal access to them.

OCCUPATIONAL MOBILITY AND FORMAL TRAINING

With the preceding overview of the rather complex structure of health services employment in mind we can turn to an analysis of the role of conventional training structures in facilitating entry and advancement. Included are employer training, vocational high schools, private technical schools, community colleges, and senior colleges or universities.

Hospitals, as we already noted, are the largest employers in the industry. They are also important training institutions. Every hospital provides brief on-the-job training (OJT) to all newly hired aides. Hospitals also operate nursing schools for both licensed practical and registered nurses. There are 25 hospitals in New York City with schools to train registered nurses; 5 hospitals have LPN programs. Students at hospital nursing schools generally pay tuition fees varying widely around an average of $500 per year. They receive no wages, but scholarships or loans are generally available for those in need. They are provided classroom instruction in special facilities at the hospital or at a cooperating college. The LPN programs are one year long, while RN programs last two to three years. After graduation students are not obligated to work at the hospital administering the program, but many are offered jobs and accept them.

The trend has been for hospitals to play a declining role in the training of nurses while the colleges assume a greater responsibility. This shift has been especially apparent in New York because the N.Y. State Nurses Association has endorsed the concept and the CUNY has willingly expanded nursing education as part of its overall growth. In addition the costs of hospital schools have increasingly exceeded the benefits received in terms of student services, with the result that hospitals have not sought to expand their programs. Nevertheless, more than half of all professional nursing students in New York City are still enrolled in hospital-based schools.

Hospitals also share responsibility with community colleges for the training of X-ray technicians. Twelve of the fifteen X-ray training programs in the city are in hospitals, but the total capacity of the hospital programs is about equal to the community college enrollment (183 students in 1970). Even when programs are administered by a college, cooperating hospitals are needed for practical experience since the state requires that a minimum of 1400 X-rays be performed by the student in a supervised setting.

The hospital also plays an important role in the training of laboratory personnel. Aides receive informal OJT and acquire skills which, combined with formal course work at a community college or private school, enable some of them to become licensed technicians by passing an examination given by the City Health Department. Hospitals also administer formal two-year training programs for laboratory technicians whose graduates need not take an exam to receive the technician's license. For medical technologist positions hospitals provide trainee slots for those with college degrees in a basic science; thirteen hospitals in New York City have AMA approved programs for those completing three years of college who wish to spend one year in the hospital to become certified technologists.

Some allied health professionals receive hospital-based training. While most of these programs are offered at colleges, the occupational and physical therapy courses have practical experience requirements which necessitate hospital affiliations for the colleges.

In the food-service department the hospital provides OJT for all newly hired aides. There is little or no training for supervisory workers, who may be drawn from a related industry (for example, commercial or school cafeterias), a community college management program, or the independent New York Institute of Dietetics. Three hospitals in New York City offer dietetic internship programs for those with a BA degree who wish to become registered with the American Dietetic Association. Membership in the Association and the professional status it represents can also be achieved by experience, and many BA's are employed immediately as dieticians without the year of intern training.

The city's vocational high schools play a far smaller role in the training of health manpower. The programs are a tenth-grade orientation course enrolling 1,049 students in 1970 and subsequent training as auxiliary health assistant (559), licensed practical nurse (671), physician's assistant (183), dental assistant (183), and in dental laboratory processing (115) and optical mechanics (16). Graduates or drop-outs from the health assistant program who enter the industry are generally employed as aides and receive additional OJT at the hospital which hires them. Students completing the practical nursing program are eligible for the state exam, but many go on to community college RN programs. Students graduating from physician or dental office assistant programs are able to find employment in the appropriate professional's office. Those studying dental mechanics may be placed in the industry but generally require additional training on the job. Those in optical mechanics are likely to find their training less useful since completion of a community college program is usually a prerequisite for a license and employment in this field.

In brief, the bulk of vocational high school training, that for aides, is useless because it provides the students with no special qualifications and leads them only to the jobs for which they would be eligible anyway. Other programs, such as those in dental mechanics or for office assistants, give the students an advantage in securing a position for which others might also qualify. Finally, the LPN program gives its graduates a distinct set of credentials which can lead them to satisfactory jobs.

The several private schools in New York City specializing in health careers are open to students with a high school education. They offer a variety of day and evening courses for medical office personnel, laboratory assistants, and laboratory technicians. The first two types of courses are generally filled with recent high school graduates. The school provides them with whatever basic skills are required and assists them in finding a related job. Evening courses in laboratory techniques are generally patronized by employed assistants who are preparing to take the city's licensing exam for technicians. In this limited way the private schools are providing an upgrading opportunity for those who can afford it. One private school, the New York Dietetics Institute, offers programs that may enable students to find jobs at a supervisory level in food-service operations at hospitals, schools, or catering services.

The community colleges in New York City train several categories of health workers. As Table 4.5 indicates, the largest group are those in nursing programs. Graduates are qualified to take the state RN exam and generally find jobs as staff nurses without difficulty. Those completing the medical lab technology program receive a New York City laboratory technician license and are hired for these positions. The dental hygiene program is geared to the state licensing requirements and graduates are qualified to work as hygienists in dental offices. Those completing the dental lab technology program are considered qualified to take positions in dental laboratories. Since we have not examined the nature of employment in dental labs, which constitute only a small part of the total industry, it is inappropriate to comment about the suitability of this course. In the absence of any formal professional or legal

Table 4.5   Enrollment in New York City Community Colleges, 1970

	Number of Colleges	Number of Students
Total — All programs	7	36,324
Total — Non-transfer programs	7	17,921
Total — Health programs	7	5,039
Nursing	7	3,443
Medical Lab Technology	5	629
Dental Hygiene	2	227
Dental Lab Technology	1	89
X-ray Technology	3	183
Ophthalmic Dispensing	1	59
Medical Emergency	2	163
Inhalation Therapy	1	67
Medical Records	1	47
Mental Health	2	132

SOURCE: City University of New York, "Enrollment Report, Fall Semester, 1970," Table IX, pp. 13-14.

requirements for such positions and the general practice of OJT, a two-year degree program may produce over-trained individuals. The three x-ray technology programs are designed to meet state licensing requirements and graduates can easily find jobs in the industry. The program in ophthalmic dispensing qualifies students for the state optician's exam, passage of which enables them to become employed in the field. The medical emergency program is designed to bring males into what is a highly female industry. It is anticipated that graduates will be able to find jobs equivalent to staff nurse positions, but working on ambulances or in the emergency room rather than in the traditional nursing services. The inhalation therapy and medical records curricula are new programs providing specialized training in fields which are in great demand.

It should be noted that a significant fraction of the community college enrollment is in evening programs. For example, over 500 nursing students, 60 dental hygiene students, and 35 medical lab technology students are attending courses at night. These courses provide an opportunity for those employed in the industry to qualify for advanced positions, and many of the evening students are working during the day in related occupations.

Senior colleges, both public and private, train several categories of allied health workers. There are special degree programs for physical therapists, occupational therapists, home economists (dietetics), medical technologists, pharmacists, and social workers. In addition BA programs in nursing are available which prepare students for the RN license. All of the above programs are primarily for full-time students, and graduates easily enter their chosen field.

OCCUPATIONAL MOBILITY AND GOVERNMENT TRAINING PROGRAMS

In the 1960's a number of federal programs were introduced and implemented to supplement the ongoing system of training for health manpower. Two broad types of legislation may be identified—that designed especially to expand the supply in specified allied health occupations and that designed to provide remedial training to assist the unemployed and underemployed.

While our interest is primarily in the second type of program, it is worth noting the nature of programs designed especially to deal with the shortages in the health services industry. The Health Professions Educational Assistance Act of 1963 covered the fields of medicine, dentistry, osteopathy, optometry, and podiatry. Grants were made to approved professional schools to improve their programs and to establish loan and scholarship funds for needy students. The Nurse Training Act of 1964 provided financial assistance to schools and students of professional nursing (RN). Special assistance was available to diploma (hospital) schools which expanded their enrollment. The Allied Health Professions Training Act of 1966 provided grants to colleges, junior colleges, or universities offering at least three different degree programs in health-related professions such as X-ray technology, medical lab technology, dental hygiene, and others. Basically, these acts provide grants to existing training structures to improve and expand their programs and to assist needy students. Appropriations have been relatively small and the impact of the programs has not been great.

The remedial training program which has had the greatest impact upon the health services industry is the Manpower Development and Training Act of 1962 (MDTA). Its two basic provisions are those for institutional training and for OJT. For institutional training in New York City the program has relied almost exclusively on the City Board of Education. The training is conducted at a variety of school facilities including special adult training center. Between 1964 and 1970 health occupations accounted for about 10 percent of the program's 34,286 trainees. The largest single category has been practical nursing with 1,851 enrollees. The MDT program constitutes a new and sizeable source of trained practical nurses. Since most training in this field is conducted in high schools, this new program offers a unique opportunity for adults to qualify for the licensing exam.

Of special significance is the LPN upgrading program which has trained 468 individuals. It is federally funded and jointly sponsored by the New York City Department of Hospitals and the municipal employees union (District Council 37 of the AFSCME); training is provided by the Board of Education. Employed aides are given released time to attend classes which are coordinated with their working experience. This represents the only such opportunity of its kind. The exceptionally small drop-out rate indicates that upgrading training for nurse aides, heretofore unavailable, could be a new and important source of LPNs.

Training programs for orderlies, which have enrolled over 900 people, are less successful and less useful. Few skills are required for this job and hospitals generally prefer brief OJT. Classroom training outside the hospital is unnecessary and does not provide any opportunities which would be available without the training. Inhalation therapist and surgical technician are new and relatively small programs with only about 60 trainees. Individuals performing these functions in the past were generally nurse aides trained by their supervisors for the specific tasks. The hospitals may welcome outside formal training, but no data are available to determine if the trainees are employed at these specialized jobs.

No broad generalizations can be made about MDTA institutional training. Much of it, primarily the training of orderlies, is wasted effort. The program has been an important new source of practical nurses and is innovating in providing formal training for new subprofessional jobs.

On-the-job training under the MDTA is administered nationally. The program provides payments to employers to cover the added costs of training employees whom they otherwise would not hire. Funds also have been made available to cover the added costs of training already hired employees for advanced positions for which they otherwise would not qualify. Hospitals may use their own staff as instructors or hire outside specialists. Since the initiation and implementation of the JOBS program in 1969, the MDTA on-the-job training program has been curtailed and little has been done in local hospitals.

Between 1967 and 1969, most federally funded OJT in the health services was supported through a contract with a national nonprofit corporation, the Social Development Corporation, which subcontracted with hospitals throughout the nation. About 5,000 trainees were enrolled in the New York area. Much of the training was for entry-level jobs for which employers have traditionally provided their own training. This includes training for housekeeping workers, food service workers, and nurse aides. It is difficult to justify this subsidized training on the grounds that the individuals would not have been hired without the added federal incentive. We have already noted that the majority of these employees are minority group members who need at a maximum only eight years of education. Since the established practice for these occupational groups is the hiring of disadvantaged workers with subsequent employer-sponsored training, federal efforts have functioned primarily as a subsidy to normal hospital operations.

Some MDTA training funds were used to finance innovative training in the New York City municipal hospitals. Over 500 aides were upgraded to newly created titles in fields of inhalation therapy, and surgical and obstetrical technology. Since this first upgrading effort, District Council 37, the municipal hospital employee's collective bargaining agent, has sought regular employer-financed training opportunities and the Hospitals Department (now Hospitals Corporation) has provided money for some additional upgrading efforts.

Other government training programs have not played a significant role in the health services industry. There are no occupation or industry breakdowns for placements in the Neighborhood Youth Corps programs, but this effort is generally considered to provide only work experience, at best, and too frequently merely income supplementation. The Job Opportunities in the Business Sector (JOBS) program, as its name implies, has concentrated on occupations in private industry and not in public or nonprofit organizations such as hospitals.

The neighborhood health centers sponsored by the Office of Economic Opportunity (OEO) have assumed training responsibilities and have produced a new category of worker—the family health worker. These individuals have served a new and useful function at the centers by providing liaison between physicians and patients, easing the professional workload, and assisting clients in securing all required services. Few similar positions exist in traditional health facilities, and few advancement opportunities exist in the centers themselves, so that family health workers have had to register in conventional training programs in order to achieve further occupational mobility. For example, the Training Department of the Martin Luther King, Jr., Neighborhood Health Center has concentrated on registering its family health workers in community college programs and is seeking to establish a school for training X-ray technicians in cooperation with its affiliated hospitals.[5]

[5] Martin Luther King Health Center, *Third Annual Report*, December 31, 1969, pp. 70–100.

TRAINING AND THE EXPANSION OF UPGRADING OPPORTUNITIES

This review of the health services industry has found that approximately two-thirds of all jobs within the hospital have entrance requirements which do not call for any specialized skills. Since hospitals have hired and will continue to hire individuals without any special skills for these jobs, new training efforts in these areas will serve no useful purpose. At the other extreme is the one job in ten which requires years of advanced training at specialized institutions.

There is a segment of hospital employment constituting about 20 to 25 percent of the total to which new and conventional training structures can be linked. Generally, each of these occupations requires a unique set of skills which must be acquired through supervised experience supplemented with classroom instruction. For such jobs as staff nurse, lab technician, X-ray technician, and physical therapist, training is a real concern.

These jobs have several common characteristics which should be noted. First, they generally require some formal accreditation. Either a license issued by the city or state or a diploma issued by a recognized institution is a prerequisite to employment. Second, these credentials are dependent upon not merely an examination, but upon attendance for some specified period of time at an approved training program. These specified courses are frequently open only to those willing to devote full time to study. Finally, these occupations are presently experiencing what employers consider to be shortages.

Given the set of circumstances we have described, what can those interested in using training as a device to enhance job mobility do? Both long and short run strategies can be identified.

For the near future it is important to concentrate training opportunities on the intermediate-level positions for which they are relevant. Most of the existing training is designed for those who are able to attend school full time. With the expansion of the City University and especially the community colleges, it is likely that the number of such openings will continue to expand. Policies of open admission and free tuition will put these opportunities within reach of almost all high school graduates.

While opportunities for full-time students are likely to expand, the same is not true for adults who are employed or underemployed in the industry. There is a need to develop part-time opportunities for intermediate level jobs which adults could patronize while still maintaining an income from their present positions. For those working in the industry it may be possible to accelerate the training process by giving course credit for relevant experience. Some steps in this direction have already been taken. The federally funded programs for nurse aides and practical nurses have followed this upgrading principle, and the municipal workers' union has negotiated a training fund, supported by Department of Hospitals contributions, which will finance remedial training designed to bring employees up to the minimum reading and arithmetic levels required for entry into nursing programs. The union active in voluntary hospitals, Local 1199, has established a training fund to support members who wish to enroll in a formal program. The support of adults entering training and the development of part-time training opportunities can help to increase occupational mobility in the health services industry.

Occupations for which part-time training might permit greater mobility for aides include nursing and technician positions. Workers now find it difficult to make these moves because recognized training programs leading to appropriate credentials are not structured to accept part-time students, and hospital personnel practices do not allow for released time for training. Expansion of part-time training might make it possible for nurse aides starting at $4,550 to move into staff nurse positions paying up to $11,500; or for a laboratory aide beginning at $5,150 to become a technologist earning over $8,000 per year. The result could be an increased percent of lower-level workers who experience upward mobility and an increased percent of better paying jobs which are staffed through upgrading.

Another possibility for the near future is to use training to develop new intermediate level jobs. Technological advances and the proliferation of diagnostic tests and instruments have created a demand for those with very specialized skills—electrocardiogram technicians, electroencephalograph technicians, inhalation therapy assistants, surgical technicians, and many more. By cooperating with hospitals to train individuals for these task, training institutions can help create new jobs

61

with a moderate skill requirement that would be open to lower-level employees.

At a broader level there are two strategies which could increase advancement opportunities in the health services industry. First, it is desirable to begin to reverse the trend toward specific educational and program requirements for licensure or professional recognition. The guarantee of quality and consumer protection for which licensure is designed might be achieved equally as well by open examinations. This would give recognition to skills acquired in a variety of settings not limited only to formal programs approved by professional associations. To ensure that examinations tested the skills needed to perform a given job, and neither more nor less, the statutes should be enforced by representatives of the consuming public as well as the particular practitioners and other professionals.

The practices of licensing bodies could also be improved in a variety of ways suggested by researchers from the Educational Testing Service. Their review of licensing practices in several states, including New York, found that few boards make an effort to inform potential applicants of the requirements and procedures for licensure, that licensing tests place a heavy emphasis on recall of facts and small details and ignore the significant advances made in the field of educational measurement during the past half-century, and that some boards are prepared to license all applicants who can demonstrate their proficiency, while others are using tests as a device for exclusion.[6] Improvement of practices followed by licensing bodies could help reduce the barriers to occupational mobility.

A second long-run possibility for enhancing job mobility is the development of new structures for the delivery of health services. The increasing emphasis on comprehensive ambulatory care and better care for the aged may lead to the growth of specialized structures such as neighborhood clinics and home-care programs. These new programs and

---

[6] Benjamin Shimberg and John Moe, *A Pilot Study to Determine the Feasibility of Investigating Nationally the Impact of Licensing Practices on the Availability and Mobility of Non-Professional Manpower in Occupations Where Skill Shortages Exist* (Princeton: Educational Testing Service, May, 1968), pp. 75, 76, 78.

structures are likely to be a source of training as well as a source of demand for manpower with a set of skills differing from those required by conventional hospital services. They may be a source of desirable jobs for which training is relevant. Future organizational changes may be even more important than technological changes in reshaping the industry's occupational structure.

5

The Construction Industry

OVERVIEW OF THE INDUSTRY

Approximately 3,400,000 of the nation's workers are engaged in construction activity. They are employed by one of three types of firms: general contractors performing building construction, general contractors engaged in nonbuilding construction, and special trade contractors. Most large-scale construction is performed under the supervision of a general contractor who subcontracts to separate special trade contractors for plumbing, heating, electrical, and other specialized types of work. In some cases a firm seeking only limited improvements contracts directly with a special trade contractor performing the type of work desired.

In New York City the industry employs an average of over 100,000 workers. More than 70 percent of these individuals work for special trade contractors, about 20 percent for general building contractors, and the remainder for nonbuilding general contractors. There are no local data on the occupational structure of the industry, and the most recent national figures are those from the 1960 census (see Table 5.1). The largest occupational groups are those that are normally considered to be the industry's workforce—craftsmen, laborers and apprentices. These are also almost exclusively male occupations.

Table 5.1 Occupational Structure of the Construction Industry

Occupation	Number of Workers	Percent of Total	Percent Female
Professional, Technical and Kindred	167,170	5.5%	2.6%
Managers, Officials, and Proprietors	147,621	4.8	3.3
Clerical and Kindred	152,944	5.0	66.5
Sales Workers	11,236	.4	8.7
Service Workers	19,188	.6	23.0
Craftsmen and Foremen	1,893,134	61.8	.4
foremen	95,547	3.1	.2
carpenters	480,914	15.7	.3
painters	156,053	5.1	1.2
pipetrades	147,139	4.8	.3
excavators	141,362	4.6	.2
brickmasons & related	127,156	4.2	.3
all others	744,963	24.3	.2
Laborers & Helpers	620,761	20.3	.6
Apprentices	24,496	.8	.7
pipetrades	6,544	.2	–
electricians	5,251	.2	1.1
carpenters	5,200	.2	–
bricklayers & related	2,450	.1	.8
all others	5,051	.1	2.0
TOTAL	3,062,038	100.0	4.3

SOURCE: U.S. Bureau of the Census, *U.S. Census of Population, 1960*, Subject Reports, Occupation by Industry, Final Report PC(2)-7C (Washington, D.C., 1963) Table 2, pp. 12-16.

Each of the major categories consists of numerous specific occupations. Over 35 different types of craftsmen are listed in the original census figures, including glaziers, roofers, elevator constructors, marble setters, and paperhangers. But over half of all craftsmen are in the five largest groups listed in Table 5.1. Similarly, among apprentices a few occupations account for most of the workers, even though a wide variety of apprenticeable trades exists.

Wages in the construction industry are high. According to the Bureau of Labor Statistics, in January 1971 union laborers in New York City received a basic wage of $6.35 per hour. Basic rates for union craftsmen ranged between $5.60 for painters and $7.25 per hour for bricklayers. In addition to these basic rates workers receive contributions on their behalf to union welfare funds which pay for insurance, pensions, and other benefits. The welfare fund payments average between one and two dollars per hour for the various crafts. Wages in the nonunion sector of the industry are somewhat lower, but most new construction in New York is performed by union contractors.

The high hourly wage scales do not always result in high annual wages for construction workers because of the intermittent nature of employment in the industry. Seasonal variations in the demand for labor and frictional unemployment caused by the relatively short periods spent by craftsmen on any one construction site prevent many men from having steady year-round work. Data gathered by the Bureau of Labor Statistics from union pension fund records in four cities covering 13 trades indicated that the average number of hours worked was low for all occupations.[1] The median hours worked for all crafts was between 987 and 1010 annually. There was considerable variation among the areas and occupations, but even in Southern California where climate was least important only 13 percent of the carpenters, 16 percent of the cement masons, and 31 percent of the operating engineers had more than 1800 hours of work during the year.

Unions, organized along craft lines, are the central manpower institition in the industry. Contractors usually do not recruit workers themselves but rely on the union to supply qualified workers as they are needed. Thus, the union is often in the position to determine who shall be considered qualified for employment and who shall be assigned to jobs that become available. Skilled workers who are not union members may be granted temporary permits by the union, but members are given priority in assigning work. The effect of these union "hiring hall" arrangements is to make union membership the key to steady employment in the industry and to give unions control over the labor supply.

[1] Bureau of Labor Statistics, *Seasonality and Manpower in Construction*, Bulletin 1642 (Washington, D.C., 1970), chap. VIII; also, Daniel Q. Mills, "A Study of Manpower Utilization in the Construction Industry: Intermittency of Employment, Unemployment, and Labor Shortages" (Manpower Administration, May, 1969).

OCCUPATIONAL MOBILITY

As the preceding discussion makes clear, entry into the construction industry on a steady basis is dependent upon acceptance into a labor union. There are several ways to secure membership in a craft union. Apprenticeship accounts for many new entrants and is of special importance because former apprentices frequently become foremen or independent contractors. Admission to an apprenticeship program is usually limited to younger individuals and takes place shortly after graduation from high school or separation from the armed forces. Some potential applicants may spend a short time working as a laborer or helper before applying for or actually beginning an apprenticeship.

Qualifications for admission to selected apprenticeship programs in New York City are presented in Table 5.2. As these data indicate, most apprentices must have finished high school and be in their late teens or early twenties. Several unions, including the plumbers, steamfitters,

Table 5.2 **Minimum Qualifications for Selected Apprenticeship Programs in New York City**

Local Craft Union	Grade Completed	Age	Test Required
Bricklayers Local 34	12	17–21[a]	No
Carpenters District Council	12	17–25	Yes
Electricians Local 3	12	18–21	Yes
Ironworkers Local 40	10	18–28	Yes
Ironworkers Local 580	12	18–25	No
Metal Lathers Local 46	12	18–25	No
Painters District Council 9	12	18–25	No[b]
Plasterers Local 60	9	18–21[a]	No
Cement Masons Local 780	8	18–21[a]	No
Plumbers Local 1	12	17–21[a]	No
Plumbers Local 2	12	18–21[a]	Yes
Roofers Local 8	12	18–30	No
Sheetmetal Workers Local 28	11	18–23[a]	No
Steamfitters Local 638	12	18–24[a]	Yes

SOURCE: F. Ray Marshall and Vernon M. Briggs, *Equal Apprenticeship Opportunities: The Nature of the Issue and the New York Experience* (Ann Arbor: Institute of Labor and Industrial Relations, 1968) pp. 6–7.

[a] – age limit higher for veterans
[b] – letter of reference required

electricians, and carpenters, require that candidates pass a special test. Competition is stiff; successful candidates for apprenticeship tend to be better qualified than many outsiders imagine. For example, the Workers Defense League, a group seeking to expand the participation of minorities in apprenticeship programs, studied the background of 65 sheet-metal apprentices and found that only four did not have a high school diploma and that 25 had spent between one and five semesters in college. Similarly, a national survey of a sample of apprentices in the pipetrades (plumbers and steamfitters) found that not only had most completed high school, but that 20 percent had some post-high school education. In addition, the study found: "Most of the men who were selected to serve apprenticeships had completed an ample number of the type of courses normally required for entry into college."[2]

Apprenticeships vary in length among the trades, but most last between three and four years. Apprentices generally start at wages about half those of journeymen and receive periodic increases which bring them up to journeyman scale at the end of the program. The latest available figures (1969) for apprenticeship programs in the construction trades in New York State indicate that 1,895 individuals completed apprenticeships during the year; 1,596 left the program without completing it. The noncompletion figures cannot be identified with "dropouts" because they include departures for military service, discharges, and out-of-state transfers, as well as those who voluntarily left the program. In some cases individuals leave before completing an apprenticeship because they can qualify for journeyman status by taking a test without completing the program.

Apprenticeship accounts for only a fraction of all journeymen. The proportion varies from trade to trade and in some cases is relatively small. No precise data are available, but the situation in New York probably does not differ significantly from that in Detroit, where the state Civil Rights Commission has prepared estimates.[3] The percent of

---

[2] Alfred S. Drew, *Educational and Training Adjustments in Selected Apprenticeable Trades* (Purdue University, November, 1969), ch. 1, p. 29.

[3] The data are presented in Dennis Derryck, "Breakthrough in the Building Trades," in National Manpower Policy Task Force, *Conference on Upgrading and New Careers* (Washington: National Manpower Policy Task Force, March, 1970).

journeymen entering through apprenticeship is high for electricians (70 percent) and plumbers (75 percent), but in two of the largest crafts, carpenters and painters, the figures are between 5 and 15 percent. In many other trades apprenticeship accounts for only about half the craftsmen.

What are the routes besides apprenticeship that individuals follow in order to qualify as a craftsman in a construction union? Several alternative means of skill acquisition are relied upon. One is the practice of "stealing a trade" while working as a laborer or helper.

As Table 5.1 revealed, more than one of every five workers in the industry is a laborer, and the proportion is even higher if one considers only the blue collar labor force. Laborers are hired without any special skill requirements. They handle the tools and materials with which craftsmen work and have opportunities to observe and practice the skills of the trades. This informal process operates in many of the specific trades. Oilers who assist operating engineers learn how to operate the equipment through informal instruction; a carpenter's helper learns in much the same way, and laborers working with masons have similar opportunities. Such arrangements exist in each of the trades. Laborers are likely to be first "upgraded" to skilled jobs during the summer when construction activity is at its peak. Employment in the industry varies by about 20 percent between February and July, and the result is a seasonal shortage of skilled workers in the summer months. During this period a helper may be granted temporary permission by a union to work as a craftsman. After doing this for one or more summers a laborer may find permanent employment at a higher level and gain admission to the union.

Other variations on this upgrading process are common. Rather than moving from a laborers union to a craft union, a worker may acquire his skills in the nonunion sector of the industry (primarily rehabilitation), and then through either union organization or personal application gain admission to a craft union.

Another possible route to journeyman status is to acquire skills in a related industry and subsequently transfer to construction activity. This route is most likely to be followed in fields such as carpentry and painting, where a sizeable percentage (about 20 percent) of those in the occupation are employed outside the construction industry. The most important source of experience is maintenance work. Skilled workers in maintenance may be drawn to construction because of the higher wage levels which prevail there.

Another source of informal training and experience is working with operative builders, who are not defined as part of the contract construction industry under the Standard Industrial Classification system. These are firms which construct homes for subsequent sale rather than under contract. Most of this small-scale residential construction is nonunion, but workers may later transfer to union contractors. It also provides an opportunity for an ambitious union craftsman to leave contract work and establish himself as an independent businessman. It is also likely that some workers enter a craft after obtaining experience during military service. A study of construction workers in upstate New York found that a small but significant number of carpenters had acquired skills in the Navy Construction Battalion (Seabees) and operating engineers who had entered their crafts via experience with the Army Corps of Engineers.[4] In many cases where skills have been acquired in other industries it may be necessary for a worker to serve for some time as a helper on construction jobs before he is granted permanent journeyman status.

The Social Security data for mobility patterns in the construction industry are presented in Table 5.3 and Table 5.4. Data are included only for males, since they comprise nearly 100 percent of all workers in the occupations with which we are concerned. The figures indicate that inter-industry mobility is quite common. Slightly more than half of those working in the industry in 1962 were not working in construction in 1966, and even in the highest earnings categories, 35 percent to 40 percent of the workers left the industry. Much of this mobility is probably involuntary and results from the sharp decline in male employment in the industry in New York over the four-year period (from 155,000 in 1962 to 119,400 in 1966). It is surprising to find that

[4] Howard G. Foster, *Labor Supply in the Construction Industry: A Case Study of Upstate New York* (PhD dissertation, Cornell University, 1969); Also, Howard Foster, "Nonapprentice Sources of Training in Construction," *Monthly Labor Review* (February, 1970), pp. 21–26.

CONSTRUCTION INDUSTRY

Table 5.3   The 1966 Status of Males Working in the New York City Construction
Industry in 1962 by Their 1962 Income

1962 Income	Percent of Total	Percent in Industry in 1966	Percent of Stayers Moving Up
$1-999	9%	23%	64%
1,000-1,999	8	20	79
2,000-2,999	8	26	65
3,000-3,999	9	39	60
4,000-4,999	9	51	66
5,000-5,999	9	54	41
6,000-6,999	9	57	37
7,000-7,999	10	61	42
8,000-8,999	9	59	50
9,000-9,999	7	66	57
10,000-14,999	11	70	19
15,000 & over	2	65	*
Total – percent	100	49	45
– number	1,550	761	345

*denotes less than one-half of one percent

Table 5.4   Characteristics of Males Working in the New York City Construction
Industry in 1966 by Their 1966 Income

1966 Income	Percent of Total	Percent in Industry in 1962	Percent Upgraded since 1962	Percent Negro
$1-999	8%	29%	*	27%
1,000-1,999	7	35	3	16
2,000-2,999	7	41	9	19
3,000-3,999	8	53	12	25
4,000-4,999	7	46	13	16
5,000-5,999	9	55	15	15
6,000-6,999	10	61	21	8
7,000-7,999	9	51	30	9
8,000-8,999	6	58	42	4
9,000-9,999	8	68	53	3
10,000-14,999	18	78	48	4
15,000 & over	5	79	54	*
Total – percent	100	56	27	12
– number	1,194	674	317	139

*denotes less than one-half of one percent

71

despite this decline in demand new entrants joined the industry in large numbers and accounted for almost 45 percent of the industry's male labor force in 1966. Even in the upper income categories new entrants were a substantial portion of all workers. There appears to be a steady and significant flow of manpower into and out of all levels of the construction industry.

The figures for workers in the four highest income levels, who represent over one-third the industry's male labor force, are an indication of the sources of skilled craftsmen. Between 20 and 40 percent are new entrants to the industry and are likely to have gained experience in a related field. The remainder are experienced workers, most of whom have advanced from lower level positions.

Table 5.4 indicates that approximately 12 percent of the total male labor force is Negro; however, there are no Negroes in the highest income category and there was subtaintial underrepresentation at income levels of $8,000 and above. This reflects the concentration of Negro construction workers in laborer positions and their lack of access to craftsmen positions.

TRAINING AND OCCUPATIONAL MOBILITY

Formal training is of little significance in the construction industry. Although some apprenticeship programs require a high school diploma, that is the only case in which educational requirements are set for entry into the industry. Upgrading depends upon formal training only to the extent that apprenticeship has such a component. In some programs the classroom segment may not be mandatory, but in others, such as electrical work or plumbing, it is crucial. Since in many trades apprenticeship supplies only a minority of the journeymen, a majority of craftsmen have had no formal instruction since they left public school. A 1963 survey found that less than 40 percent of all construction craftsmen had *ever* had *any* formal training, and less than 20 percent named formal training as the most helpful way of acquiring their trade (see Table 5.5). The majority of journeymen learned their skills through on-the-job training and casual experiences.

Other than apprenticeship, the only opportunities in New York City for formal instruction in the construction trades are vocational high

Table 5.5   Training Experience of Construction Craftsmen (percentage distribution)

	Total	No Training Needed	Formal Training	OJT	Casual Methods	Not Available
Type of Training Ever Experienced[a]						
Total – all construction	100.0%	1.7%	39.4%	54.8%	57.2%	.9%
Brickmasons & related	100.0	2.5	44.7	56.6	53.5	–
Carpenters	100.0	2.8	31.1	48.7	67.8	.6
Electricians	100.0	–	72.9	71.2	33.4	–
Excavating & related	100.0	2.2	11.2	47.0	72.2	1.0
Painters	100.0	1.9	27.8	46.9	58.7	.5
Pipetrades	100.0	.7	55.0	66.6	39.1	2.6
Sheetmetal & related	100.0	–	70.9	58.1	44.4	1.7
All others	100.0	1.1	34.1	59.1	68.8	2.3
Most Helpful Type of Training						
Total – all construction	100.0%	1.7%	17.5%	27.9%	33.9%	19.0%
Brickmasons & related	100.0	2.5	19.5	29.0	28.3	20.8
Carpenters	100.0	2.8	11.7	25.4	44.0	16.2
Electricians	100.0	–	36.1	29.0	9.9	24.9
Excavating & related	100.0	2.2	3.8	26.8	52.7	14.4
Painters	100.0	1.9	17.9	25.0	38.7	16.0
Pipetrades	100.0	.7	19.3	37.4	17.6	25.1
Sheetmetal & related	100.0	–	28.3	26.5	29.1	16.2
All others	100.0	1.1	18.2	29.0	27.2	24.4

[a]–Totals may exceed 100 percent because individuals experience more than one type of training.

SOURCE: *Formal Occupational Training of Adult Workers*, Manpower Automation Research Monograph no. 2 (U.S. Dept. of Labor, December, 1965) Table 11, pp. 43–44.

school programs and special federally funded programs intended to increase minority participation in the building trades. Training in the high schools is available in carpentry, electrical work, plumbing, and sheetmetal work. Total enrollment in these programs is over 3,000, about two-thirds of which is in electrical training. This instruction is of extremely limited utility, since it does not qualify graduates for advanced placement in the industry; they must compete on an equal footing with all others for apprenticeship openings. Since apprentice admission procedures often include tests of academic ability and aptitude, these vocational high school graduates are at a disadvantage when competing with other high school graduates.

The Joint Apprenticeship Program of the Workers' Defense League and the A. Philip Randolph Educational Fund (JAP) is an organization that has sponsored a pre-apprenticeship program to inform members of minority groups of opportunities in the construction industry and to help them qualify for employment in the industry.[5] The program began under private sponsorship in 1964 and has been funded by the Department of Labor since 1967. In New York City, field offices in Bedford-Stuyvesant and Harlem recruit young men meeting the formal requirements for apprenticeship and then provide them with special tutoring sessions designed specifically to produce high scores on the competitive exams and selection interviews.

As the data in Table 5.6 demonstrate, the JAP has successfully placed numerous individuals in each of the apprenticeable trades. They have been particularly effective in key trades, such as electrical work and the pipetrades, in which apprenticeship accounts for a large percentage of the journeymen. Since some trades are filled largely through nonapprenticeship sources, the JAP has also begun programs designed to achieve direct entry for those with related work experience.

The first such program in New York City was the East New York Model Cities Journeyman Training Program sponsored by the JAP and the New York City Manpower and Career Development Agency.[6] Contractors working in the model cities area agreed to accept experienced workers recruited by JAP or MCDA staff at levels above starting apprenticeship and to give credit towards journeyman status for their prior experience. After one year of operation the program had placed 62 individuals and 41 continued their employment. Many of those placed at advanced levels were granted journeyman status in a short time and others were working at second or third year apprentice rates in several trades.

[5] Thomas R. Brooks, *Black Builders: A Job Program that Works* (New York: League for Industrial Democracy, 1970).

[6] Eddie Johnson, *The Minority Experience in Construction: The East New York Model Cities Journeyman Training Program* (New York: The Institute of the Joint Apprenticeship Program, Workers Defense League, 1970).

CONSTRUCTION INDUSTRY

Table 5.6   Registered Apprenticeships and JAP Placements in New York State

Trade	Registered Apprenticeships[a]		JAP Placements[b]	
	Active at Year End	New Registrations	N.Y.C. Offices	N.Y.S. Offices
All Construction	10,474	4,755	1,036	1,375
Bricklayers & related	498	211	34	53
Carpenters	1,528	763	126	159
Cement Masons	60	53	2	19
Electricians	3,436	1,366	223	246
Glaziers	119	70	44	46
Lathers	152	61	15	16
Painters	294	242	106	153
Pipetrades	2,121	839	107	155
Plasterers	27	23	38	45
Roofers	104	82	22	75
Sheetmetal workers	1,362	701	112	142
All others	773	344	207	266

[a]–New York State totals for year 1969.
[b]–Cumulative total to November, 1970.

SOURCE: Data supplied by the Joint Apprenticeship Program and the United States Department of Labor.

In December of 1970 plans were announced to expand the program to include contractors throughout the city; the goal was 800 placements in the first year of operation. Once it is put into operation, this "New York Plan" may be a new source of minority journeymen. But the difficulties in recruiting qualified workers and keeping them in the program encountered in the Model Cities program may make the goal difficult to achieve. It must also be noted that several unions, particularly those representing trades in which apprenticeship is the dominant entry route, have not agreed to participate in the plan. The Model Cities and the New York Plan training program are likely to be most successful in trades such as carpentry and bricklaying where direct entry is a common source of journeymen.

It is important to note that the New York Plan is simply a training program and not a "hometown plan" for contract compliance similar to the highly publicized Philadelphia and Chicago Plans. To date the New York Plan remains a joint city and state program without any federal

75

funds or approval. A distinction should be made between contract compliance efforts and training programs. Federal regulations prohibit discrimination in employment by firms working under government contract and these provisions apply to construction contracts. Employers awarded federal contracts are required to take "affirmative action" to prevent discriminatory employment patterns. Prior to July 1969, when the Philadelphia Plan was announced, suitable affirmative action was considered to be participation in an Apprenticeship Outreach program. Under these programs, funded by the federal government and executed by unions, civil rights groups, and local employment services, efforts were made to recruit eligible Negroes for admission to apprenticeship programs. By 1970 Outreach programs existed in 54 cities under the sponsorship of such groups as the Urban League and the Workers Defense League. The JAP of the Workers Defense League in New York City, described above, is one of these programs.

The Apprenticeship Outreach approach to meeting affirmative action requirements resulted in increased minority participation in apprenticeship programs. However, because apprenticeship accounts for only a fraction of the total labor force in many crafts and because of the long duration and relatively high dropout rates in apprenticeship training, the Outreach programs did not have a substantial impact on the racial composition of the total industry workforce. The Philadelphia Plan extended affirmative action requirements beyond participation in Outreach programs. It specified numerical goals for minority employment, such as 19 percent of the workers in each covered craft, and required contractors to pledge to meet these goals and to specify the action they would take to meet them. Pledges might be met through apprenticeship placements, nonapprenticeship training programs, or the use of already qualified nonunion minority craftsmen. In some cases the percentage goals could be met by assigning to federal construction minority craftsmen previously accepted as union members and working on nongovernment contracts.

When the Secretary of Labor announced the Philadelphia Plan, he also stated that affirmative action requirements could be met in other areas through participation in voluntary "hometown plans," designed by local groups and not necessarily imposed by the federal government. Subsequently voluntary hometown plans were agreed to in Chicago,

Boston, Pittsburgh, Denver, and other cities. The plans differed significantly in both goals and methods. The Chicago Plan sought to expand minority participation by 4,000 by immediately placing on construction jobs 1,000 qualified black journeymen and by training through apprenticeship and accelerated nonapprenticeship programs another 3,000. The federal government supplied the local groups with $1 million to carry out this program. Boston contractors agreed to place 2,000 minority workers over 5 years; Denver contractors, 400 over 18 months; Pittsburgh contractors agreed to 1,250 new journeymen over 4 years. Some of the plans specified numerical goals for each craft while others left the occupational breakdown to future negotiations.

The effect of the hometown plan approach to contract compliance was to provide numerical standards by which to judge efforts and to extend the affirmative action requirements beyond apprenticeship outreach to include accelerated journeyman training programs and the immediate placement of qualified minority craftsmen drawn from outside the unionized sector of the industry. The specific nature of an acceptable affirmative action program was subject to negotiation by local groups. The results of the programs have been far less satisfactory than anticipated. Because of outright refusal to cooperate by local unions and contractors, disagreements between local civil rights groups and union or industry representatives, and the decline in construction activity in many areas, first year goals have not been met.

In New York City there is as yet no hometown plan which the federal government has accepted as meeting the affirmative action requirement for its contractors and the Secretary of Labor has not imposed one. The NAACP and other groups have opposed acceptance of the "New York Plan" as a federal hometown plan on the grounds that it specifies 800 as a maximum and not as a minimum; it does not specify the crafts to which trainees will be assigned; and it does not guarantee union membership to those completing training.[7]

As the hometown plans illustrate, there is a difference between training programs and contract compliance programs. Antidiscrimination and affirmative action clauses require not only abandonment of prior

[7]Herbert Hill, "Statement Before the New York State Advisory Committee, United States Commission on Civil Rights," March 9, 1971.

racist practices but continued efforts to achieve integration through recruitment for traditional apprenticeship programs and special accelerated training programs. Training efforts are only one facet of contract compliance requirements.

EXPANDING UPGRADING OPPORTUNITIES

Upgrading, defined as intra-industry occupational mobility, is a source of skilled manpower in all instances in which apprenticeship, experience as a helper, or work in the nonunion section qualifies men for craftsmen positions. Adding the other intra-industry sources of manpower to the estimates for apprenticeship suggests that, depending upon the craft, upgrading accounts for between 50 percent and 90 percent of the craftsmen. This estimate coincides with the Social Security figures on workers earning $8,000 and above (see Table 5.4), which indicate that between 20 percent and 40 percent of all workers at these levels have moved into construction from another industry. In sum, upgrading accounts for the majority of craftsmen in each trade and is almost the exclusive source in a few key trades. However, inter-industry mobility is an important source of manpower in several fields, the largest of which are painting and carpentry.

Logic would seem to indicate that the best way to expand upgrading opportunities is to advance lower level personnel into those trades which now rely heavily upon other sources of manpower. But two factors make this course of action impractical. First, the laborers, who are the traditional "lower level" of the industry, earn an hourly wage rate which is often higher than or almost equal to that of several trades which do not rely heavily upon upgrading. There is little incentive for laborers to move into these crafts. Second, several of the crafts relying on outside sources of manpower are those occupations which are not highly industry specific. For example, many painters and carpenters are found in maintenance work or with operative builders and many iron workers are employed by metal fabricators who install their own products. For these men movement into the construction industry does not constitute occupational mobility, although their income is likely to increase because of the higher wage rates in contract construction. Because of the high wage rates in "lower level" positions and the available supply of skilled workers in other industries, the possibilities for expanding upgrading opportunities in the construction industry are severely limited.

While the extent of upgrading may not be expanded, the process certainly can be made to operate in a less discriminatory fashion. The crucial manpower challenge in the construction industry is not to generate upgrading opportunities, but to integrate certain key trades. The Social Security data (see Table 5.4) documented the underrepresentation of Negroes in better paying jobs, and the Equal Employment Opportunity Commission figures in Table 5.7 point to the specific trades which have only a small percentage of Negroes. The largest categories with serious underrepresentation are the carpenters, electrical

Table 5.7 Total and Minority Group Membership in Construction Trade Referral Unions in the New York Area, 1969

Union	Total Membership	Percent	
		Negro	Spanish American
All building trades	67,884	10.6%	5.8%
Mechanical Trades	17,982	6.4	5.7
Electrical Workers	3,305	2.4	1.7
Iron Workers	6,683	14.0	13.2
Pipetrades	4,727	1.9	.4
Others[a]	3,267	1.3	6.2
General Construction I	31,291	7.8	3.7
Bricklayers	1,135	1.9	3.1
Carpenters	22,877	6.5	3.6
Operating Engineers	5,418	15.9	5.4
Plasterers-Masons	791	7.0	.6
Others[b]	1,070	1.2	.4
General Construction II	18,611	19.3	9.5
Laborers	13,925	21.9	9.8
Others[c]	4,686	11.8	8.9

[a]—Boilermakers, elevator constructors, and sheet metal workers.
[b]—Asbestos workers, lathers, marble, slate and stone workers, and stone cutters.
[c]—Painters, decorators, and roofers.

SOURCE: Data supplied by the U.S. Equal Employment Opportunity Commission.

workers and plumbers. Integrating these trades requires strategies suited to the prevailing entry routes. In plumbing and electrical work the vast majority of craftsmen have moved up through apprenticeship programs, so efforts to expand minority participation should concentrate upon apprenticeship placements. Pre-apprenticeship training programs can help to recruit and qualify candidates for available openings. Speedy integration will be facilitated when apprenticeship entry requirements and selection procedures which operate in a discriminatory manner are eliminated, and court battles challenging the validity of current examination content and procedure are likely. In the meantime, efforts such as the JAP can help black and Puerto Rican candidates compete successfully in the existing structure.

In fields such as carpentry, where apprenticeship accounts for only a small fraction of the journeymen, pre-apprentice training programs can have only a limited impact on the racial composition of the entire craft. Programs providing direct placement and supplementary training for partially qualified journeymen, such as the Model Cities program, are best suited to integrating these trades. The successful integration of the building trades will require the implementation of different types of programs which are tailored to the specific entry patterns that dominate in each craft.

6

Local Public Transit

OVERVIEW OF THE INDUSTRY

In New York City, local transportation services are not a direct municipal function. The only mass transit facility operated by the City of New York is the Staten Island ferry, an atypical service not included in the scope of this study. Commuter railroads, whose routes extend beyond city and state borders, are not municipal responsibilities. The Long Island Railroad, serving primarily Nassau and Suffolk counties, is owned and operated directly by the Metropolitan Transportation Authority, a state-chartered, independent body. A private railroad, the Penn Central, owns and operates the other major commuter lines in the area.

While the City operates no land mass transit facilities, it does retain ownership to a vast subway and bus system and each year allocates over $130 million of its capital budget for improvements in the systems. However, operations are the responsibility of the New York City Transit Authority (TA) and its subdivision, the Manhattan and Bronx Surface Transit Operating Authority. The former runs the subway systems, the latter, the bus routes. Both are under the general jurisdiction of the Metropolitan Transportation Authority.

The city government provides a limited subsidy to the TA operating funds by paying the salaries of a special TA police force and through payments for reduced fares granted the elderly and for free transportation given school children. The TA must follow broad guidelines set forth by the New York City Civil Service Commission, but it has its own personnel department and functions as an independent body in dealing with most manpower problems and policies.

The TA is the basic unit in the "industry" and this investigation is limited to this organization. As of July, 1970, the TA employed a total of 42,824 individuals. The workers were distributed among several functional divisions in the following manner:

Rapid Transit Transportation 8,368
Maintenance of Way 6,728
Car Maintenance 6,698
Surface Transit 6,047
Stations 5,739
Surface Maintenance 1,695
Power 1,044
Purchase 302
All Other 6,203

Total 42,824

With only a few exceptions each department has its own occupational structure. Each has its own entry level position, which is filled by an open competitive examination. The remaining jobs in the department are filled by promotion from the entry positions and subsequent intermediate level positions. Promotions are based upon closed (open only to TA employees in designated job titles) competitive examinations. Employees study for the exams primarily with books containing advice and sample questions prepared by a private publisher and sold commercially. Based on the exam scores, appointments are made, and once the employee is promoted, he receives training from the TA in his new job. This is done both on-the-job and in classroom settings. As a general rule employees are eligible to compete for promotion from one hourly rated job title to another hourly rated title after six months service in the lower position. Eligibility for advancement from an hourly rated title to an annual salary position is dependent upon at least one year of service in the appropriate hourly title.

Most occupational titles in the TA were traditionally reserved for men. Exceptions were primarily the administrative and clerical positions and some jobs in the Stations Division. However, within the last year the Authority has reversed its policy and women will be eligible for appointment and promotion to various titles in other divisions. The first female towerman, a promotional title in the Rapid Transit Division, was appointed in April of 1971 from a group of eligible railroad clerks. Similar breakthroughs are anticipated in other titles.

OCCUPATIONAL MOBILITY IN TWO DEPARTMENTS

A closer look at the occupational structure and mobility routes in the two largest departments—Rapid Transit Transportation (RTT) and Maintenance of Way (MW)—will help provide a better understanding of how this well-defined advancement system operates. They are useful examples not only for their size, but also because they represent the two basic functions of operations and maintenance.

The number of incumbents and the wage range for the basic non-administrative job titles in the RTT Department are presented in Table 6.1. Individuals enter the department as conductors. Appointment to this position is based upon an examination open to the public. There are no formal educational requirements, but candidates must pass a strict physical examination. A minimum score of 70 is required on the open competitive examination and positions are awarded to those with the highest scores above this level.

After performing successfully for six months a conductor is eligible to compete for promotion to either motorman or towerman, or after one year of service he may seek to become an assistant train dispatcher. All three positions are filled by closed competitive examinations. However, in each case conductors are not the only eligible class of TA employees. For promotion to motorman the conductor competes with bus operators; for towerman positions he competes with a category of maintainer's helper in the maintenance of way department and railroad clerks in the station department; for assistant train dispatcher positions he competes with railroad clerks and collecting agents in the station department. These RTT department positions are not the only intermediate level jobs open to the workers in other divisions. They are

Table 6.1   Selected Job Titles in the Rapid Transit Transportation Department

Job Title	Number of Employees	Wage Rate
Conductor	3,300	$3.78–4.51
Towerman	60	4.40–4.96
Motorman	3,400	4.50–5.30
Ass't Train Dispatcher	430	9,600–11,300
Yard Master	82	11,475–12,948
Train Dispatcher	315	11,475–12,948
Schedule Maker	12	11,475–12,948
Motorman Instructor	70	12,909–13,841
Trainmaster	81	13,621–15,108

eligible for promotion to additional titles within their own departments.

Almost every employee planning to take a promotional exam studies on his own with books designed specifically for the exams. Generally this preparation is sufficient for an adequate number of candidates to achieve the minimal acceptable score on the test. One notable exception is the case of Assistant Train Dispatcher, where a TA official reported that the failure rate was 95 percent and that the exam frequently did not produce enough eligible candidates to fill the openings. This position requires an ability to deal quickly and accurately with numbers and to keep precise records. Since all of those competing (conductors, railroad clerks, and collecting agents) are in job titles which have no specific educational requirements, they often have limited academic preparation and experience difficulty with the exam.

After performing satisfactorily at one of these intermediate level positions (motorman, towerman, assistant train dispatcher) an individual may compete for additional promotions. Motormen, and only motormen, are eligible for advancement to motorman instructor. Motormen and towermen compete for yardmaster positions. All three intermediate level positions may compete for train dispatcher jobs. The schedule maker title is filled from the ranks of train dispatchers and yard masters and represents only a change in title. The highest active competitive title is train master. Those in all salaried titles in the department except assistant train dispatchers compete for this position.

There is considerable opportunity for advancement in the rapid transit department. There are more motormen that conductors, so that many conductors, who start at $3.78 per hour, have a chance to move into better jobs and earn up to $5.30 per hour. A smaller group of those beginning as conductors will advance even further and move into higher level positions paying up to $15,000 per year.

Advancement in the Maintenance of Way Department follows the same basic principles as in the rapid transit department. There are five entry positions that are filled by open competitive examinations— Trackman, Maintainer's Helper A, Maintainer's Helper B, Maintainer's Helper D, and Turnstile Maintainer.

Trackmen need meet no special educational or skill requirements and after six months they are eligible to compete with Maintainer's Helpers A for power distributor maintainer jobs. A trackman with one year of experience may take the exam for foreman-track. Foremen may subsequently compete for assistant supervisor-track and supervisor-track positions. Track supervisors as well as power distributor supervisors compete for available positions as assistant superintendant-track.

Positions as Maintainer's Helper B and Maintainer's Helper D are open to those with a diploma from a vocational high school in some mechanical or related field and to all individuals, regardless of educational background, who have had four years work experience in some related area.

Table 6.2 Job Categories in the Maintenance of Way Department

Job Category	Number of Employees	Wage Rate
Maintainer's Helper A	787	$3.84–3.95
Maintainer's Helper B	48	3.84–3.95
Maintainer's Helper D	1,241	3.84–3.95
Trackman	1,711	4.12–4.82
Turnstile Maintainer	115	4.38–4.82
All other maintainers (15 separate titles)	2,550	4.38–4.82*
All foremen (15 separate titles)	641	11,475–12,948*
All assistant supervisors (11 separate titles)	71	13,269–14,023
All supervisors	32	13,621–14,364

*Slightly higher for some electrical specialties.

In addition car cleaners (an entry level title in the car maintenance department which has no special eligibility requirements) with six months of service are permitted to compete in the open exam for maintainer's helper B positions. Frequently individuals without suitable education or work experience will enter as car cleaners and after six months seek appointments in the Maintenance of Way Department.

Requirements for maintainer's helper A are similar except the vocational high school major or the four years of experience must be in electrical work or repairs. As noted earlier, maintainer's helpers A are eligible to compete for promotion to towerman in the RTT Department. In general the main sources of applicants for all classes of maintainer's helper are recent vocational high school graduates rather than older workers who qualify by right of experience.

Each category of maintainer's helper is eligible for promotion to two or more of the fifteen maintainer level jobs. These are closed promotional titles (except for turnstile maintainer), and only the appropriate category of maintainer's helper can fill them. Maintainers may move up to foreman, assistant supervisor, and supervisor within their specialty. Supervisors in some specialties may then compete for one of the three different assistant superintendent titles. Above this level positions in the Maintenance of Way Department are noncompetitive.

Several job titles in the Maintenance of Way Department also exist in the Surface Maintenance Department. Incumbents in these positions may compete for promotions in either department. For example, an individual might enter the TA as a Maintainer's Helper A in the Maintenence of Way Department and win a promotion to power distributor maintainer in the Surface Maintenance Department and then to power distributor foreman in the same department. He could still compete for promotion to assistant supervisor-power distribution in the Maintenance of Way Department along with foremen in the same specialty in the Maintenance of Way Department.

The job of turnstile maintainer differs from other maintainer specialties in the MW Department because it is open competitive and not filled from the ranks of helpers. To be eligible to compete a candidate must have at least four years of experience in repairing coin boxes, change machines, cash registers, or in a machine shop. This practice of recruiting experienced workers resembles the process for hiring maintainers of various specialties in the Car Maintenance Department. In that division there is presently no helper grade and maintainers are open competitive positions with varying types of experience required. However, the TA is now considering a trainee level position in this department with less elaborate qualifications. These trainees could advance to maintainers jobs.

The MW Department, like the RTT Department, offers considerable opportunity for occupational advancement. Most maintainer's helpers, who start at $3.84 per hour, can advance to maintainers jobs and earn up to $4.82 per hour. A smaller number will be able to move into the few supervisory positions and earn over $11,000 as a foreman or more than $14,000 as a supervisor.

Our examination of mobility within the RTT and MW Departments leads to several general conclusions. First, the TA cannot be considered as a single internal labor market. It consists of several divisions and specialties within these divisions, which have their own job progressions. At the lower levels there is a limited degree of interdepartmental mobility, but this soon disappears and does not reappear until the highest levels are reached. The relative number of promotional opportunities varies among the divisions, but in every case there are several positions into which an entering worker may advance.

Second, it is an industry in which entrance takes place almost exclusively at the lowest levels and in which higher level positions are filled entirely by promotion from within. Most of the entry positions have no formal education or training requirements and appointment is based strictly on competitive examinations. Only for some maintenance functions is experience or skill training an essential prerequisite. Foreman and supervisory positions are reserved for lower-level workers, and no one, regardless of his prior educational experience, can enter at these levels.

The competitive examinations for entry positions are generally written, multiple-choice tests. The Arco Publishing Company, a firm specializing in study guides for civil service and other standardized exams, puts out books containing prior examinations and practice questions which candidates can consult. The exams for nonmaintenance positions contain questions testing general knowledge, familiarity with the subway system, safety practices, and the ability to perform basic arithmetic operations and read simple paragraphs. For example, a recent test for railroad clerk candidates required them to find the product of 154 and 48, comprehend a short written accident report, read a train schedule, know that there was no subway stop at 42 Street and Third Avenue, identify the color of the paint used on the edge of subway platforms, and select the best reason why clerks should keep the change booth door closed and locked. The examinations for maintainer's helpers are more specialized and test primarily trade-related knowledge. For example, a recent Maintainer's Helper A exam required the candidates to define a milliampere, read diagrams and identify electrical symbols, select the safest method for determining which of two wires in a line was ungrounded, and specify the suitable device for attaching a metal box to a hollow tile wall.

Promotion is dependent upon minimal seniority requirements (six months or one year in a lower level title) and the ability to take examinations. The promotional exams are typically written, multiple-choice tests requiring general familiarity with the subway system as well as specific knowledge of Transit Authority operating and safety procedures. A recent motorman exam required candidates to know in which borough Shea Stadium is located, the meaning of a blue light on the trackway, the proper horn signal to call for a car inspector, and the voltage in the third rail of the subway system. Potential assistant train dispatchers had to know how to properly read and fill in a variety of Transit Authority forms such as schedules, pay sheets, and train registers, know the colors of switch levers and signal levers, and be able to quickly deal with problems like this one:

During the night, the headway was increased on the express service from 10 minutes to 20 minutes, and the train length was reduced from 10 cars to 6 cars. The reduction in car service per hour equals: a) 24 cars b) 32 cars c) 42 cars d) 52 cars

Quality of performance at lower level jobs, the acquisition of new skills, and the ability to do more responsible work are important only to the extent to which they are reflected in promotional exams. The face that this relationship may be slight is evidenced by the recent *Report of the Panel Appointed to Study Personnel Policies and Practices of the New York City Transit Authority*. The panel was appointed after the catastrophic subway collision of May, 1970, in which two people were killed and over 60 injured. Their investigation found that the motorman principally responsible for the accident had been promoted to his position as a result of his test scores despite the fact that he had a poor record as a conductor and had previously been demoted back to conductor because of unsatisfactory performance as a towerman. Specifically, the group concluded: "It appears that an error was made in allowing Mr. Haynes to be promoted to Motorman. His past records should have been reviewed and should have been disqualifying at the time he was being considered for a Motorman's job." This finding was the basis for one of the panel's key recommendations: "That all information relating to applicants for promotion be more thoroughly reviewed and that performance on previous jobs have as much weight in determining promotions as do various test scores."[1]

TRAINING AND OCCUPATIONAL MOBILITY

The preceding discussion of occupational mobility clearly indicates that the TA is the most important source of training for transit workers. It is the exclusive source of new skills in the promotion process and also provides significant training for those entering the system. It is only for entry positions in maintenance functions that there is some reliance upon outside sources to supply trained workers.

Often even in those cases where the entering worker must bring some special skills to his new job, other employers rather than training institutions are relied upon for preparation. Related experience in other industries is accepted for most positions having specific requirements and is the exclusive source of training for some titles. However, in many cases graduation from vocational high school may serve as an alternative to work experience, and this represents the only linkage between formal training and mobility in the TA.

There are several vocational high school curricula which might provide the background for entering TA maintenance work. There is a program in electrical installation and practices with a senior enrollment

[1] *Report of the Panel Appointed to Study Personnel Policies and Practices of the New York City Transit Authority*, March 12, 1971, pp. 2, 10; see also, C. Sidamon Eristoff, "Report to Mayor John V. Lindsay from the Transportation Administrator on the Collision and Derailment Involving Two 'GG' Trains Operating on the Queens Boulevard Line–Division B South of the Roosevelt Avenue Station on May 20, 1970, in the Borough of Queens," July 3, 1970.

of about 600. In mechanical fields there are large programs in auto mechanics (senior-year enrollment of 500), aviation mechanics (668), and machine shop practice (100). Since there are no available data on the number or percentage of high school graduates entering the TA or on the number or percentage of TA employees coming directly from vocational high schools, it is difficult to evaluate the linkage other than to note that TA officials report that many of their maintainer's helpers are coming from the high schools.

In areas other than maintenance formal training is of little significance. For most entry titles there are no educational or training requirements and the open examinations have attracted a large group of candidates and yielded an ample supply of qualified manpower. Once an individual is hired by the TA his employer will provide whatever training is required for more advanced positions.

EXPANDING UPGRADING OPPORTUNITIES

There are only limited possibilities for expanding occupational mobility in local public transit. Upgrading is presently the dominant and almost exclusive source of skilled manpower. The TA has closed and well-defined promotional sequences. Virtually all employees in intermediate and upper level positions have moved up from within their department. In addition, even at the lowest levels employment in this industry is characterized by relatively high wage rates. Entry level jobs such as maintainer's helper and conductor pay close to $4.00 per hour.

Movement into the industry could be eased through the redesign of some entry level maintainers jobs to allow for trainee (helper) positions, a step being considered by the TA. Trainees could be hired without the training or experience required of maintainers. After working under the supervision of experienced craftsmen, they would be eligible to move into the higher level positions. Job redesign may be a viable strategy in these fields.

Another approach is to provide special training for the promotional exams. At present each individual generally studies on his own. Other municipal civil service employees, particularly those in clerical and secretarial titles, have benefited from union-sponsored courses geared to the tests. However, this will add to the net amount of advancement only if current practices do not yield a sufficient number of candidates who achieve the minimum acceptable score. This is the case for few titles in the TA, but nonetheless could be helpful in instances such as promotion to assistant train dispatcher.

The promotional exams raise the broader issue of the need to re-examine criteria for promotion. Civil service systems have traditionally relied upon competitive examinations to select among the eligible candidates. The purpose is to avoid favoritism, overt discrimination, and patronage or bribery. But, as the case of the motorman involved in the 1970 subway collision demonstrated, the examinations frequently have no relationship to capabilities for performing specific tasks. In addition, there is mounting, if not conclusive, evidence that such examinations are best suited to those with white, middle-class backgrounds and consequently result in under-representation of minorities in promotional positions. While these consequences are alleged to be most pronounced in the educational system, the testing procedures in all public agencies have been open to similar charges. Yet there are no ideal promotion criteria to recommend as a replacement for competitive testing. Reliance exclusively upon seniority is generally avoided because it is likely to stifle initiative and hamper productivity. Private industry frequently relies upon the informal evaluation of supervisors in awarding promotions. While this practice gives high priority to competence in job related skills, it also is conducive to favoritism, and few would point to private industry as a model for nondiscriminatory promotional practices. There are no easy solutions for an employer (or a society) which seeks to rely upon upgrading to fill better jobs and simultaneously hopes to maintain standards of productivity and to integrate higher occupational categories. Civil service examinations are an uneasy compromise and experimentation should be encouraged.

New York City's public transit system is destined to grow rapidly in the next decade. The Mayor and the Board of Estimate have approved six new subway routes for construction and six additional routes are being planned by the TA. The anticipated cost for this program is $1.3 billion. This growth will be accompanied by substantial replacement needs generated by the generous retirement program negotiated by the

Transit Workers' Union. In July, 1968, the new program went into effect permitting retirement at half pay based on the last year's earnings after 20 years service at the age of 50. After 18 months, 5,655 experienced workers retired, leaving vacancies at all levels of the system.[2]

By taking steps to ease entry into the system, to provide its employees with the basic skills required for promotions, and to revise its promotional practices to strike an optimal compromise between equity and efficiency, the TA can adapt its existing internal labor market to successfully meet its coming manpower needs. At the same time it can provide advancement opportunities for thousands of New Yorkers.

[2] Thomas Brooks, "Subway Roulette," *New York* (June 15, 1970), pp. 41–48.

7

Upgrading Policies and Programs

Studies of the internal labor markets of five industries were undertaken in order to arrive at some tentative answers to the questions presented in the introductory chapter: What are the factors which limit the incidence and extent of upgrading among workers? Can governmental intervention help overcome these obstacles, and if so, what form of intervention is likely to be most effective? In particular, can additional public or private investment in training help workers achieve occupational mobility?

An analysis of the process of occupational mobility within selected manufacturing and service industries suggests three fundamental conclusions about the opportunities for assisting low-wage workers improve their status. First, the occupational structure of an industry is the major determinant of the availability of upgrading opportunities within the industry. Occupational structures may take a variety of forms. Industries such as retail eating and drinking places possess a sharply narrowed pyramid in which the number of better paying jobs is relatively small. In such cases upgrading opportunities are necessarily severely limited because of the small number of desirable positions relative to the total number of workers. Similarly employment in the garment industry is concentrated in the lower levels, and upgrading possibilities are restricted by the relatively few higher-wage jobs available. This is especially true for females who are presently denied access to virtually all the occupations with above average wage levels. In contrast the structure of employment in the construction industry makes possible a high degree of upgrading because of the large number of higher wage positions relative to the total workforce. First and foremost, upgrading depends upon the availability of upper level jobs, and in several industries such jobs are only a very small proportion of total employment. In such cases there is little potential for advancement for the workers in the industry.

A second conclusion to which the case studies lead is that regardless of the number or proportion of better paying positions which exist in an industry, upgrading is presently the dominant means for filling them. Analysis of the Social Security Administration data available for four of the New York City industries studied indicated that between 73 percent and 80 percent of all workers earning $8,000 or more per year had at least four years experience in their respective industries and that most of this group had moved up from positions paying substantially less during the four-year period. Upgrading is presently a key source of intermediate and higher level manpower in many industries, and there are only limited improvements to be made in increasing the proportion of better paying positions filled in this fashion.

The third basic finding is that formal training frequently is not required for occupational mobility. In only one industry, health services, did we find a substantial number of workers who required institutional instruction to qualify for their positions and apprenticeship was the dominant source of supply for only a few of the construction trades. Although formal instruction was helpful in the case of cooks and some additional construction craftsmen, in most instances workers acquired whatever skills they needed through an informal process of observation and practice-on-the-job. Few were unable to advance because they lacked the requisite skills, and inadequate training opportunities were not found to be an important obstacle to advancement.

POLICY OBJECTIVES

Building upon the concepts developed in the Introduction and the three conclusions presented above, we can describe five objectives which upgrading policy might be designed to achieve. First, one can seek to increase the total number of workers who move into better jobs. If, as has been suggested, the primary obstacle to expanding this number is the limited availability of higher level positions, then efforts should focus on altering the utilization of manpower so as to create a more favorable occupational structure. Conventional wisdom leads most observers to believe that this is a difficult goal to achieve through government manpower programs. The generally accepted explanation of occupational structures is that they are determined primarily by the nature of consumer demand, the state of existing technology, and the organizational form within an industry.

The national occupational structure is determined by the industrial mix of the economy. Since industries vary in their manpower requirements, the aggregate occupational structure is a function of the relative size of each industry. The most significant changes in the United States occupational structure have been those rooted in the shifting industrial base of the economy. These transformations, such as the continuing decline in agricultural employment and the recent growth of business and consumer services, are based on long-run trends such as the mechanization of agriculture and the changing pattern of consumer expenditures. Historically many individuals have been able to take advantage of these structural changes and move from agricultural employment to more lucrative manufacturing employment. The nation's changing industrial mix will probably continue to afford many individuals a chance to improve their earnings by moving from low wage industries to more rewarding ones. But increased upgrading opportunities are based upon manpower requirements within industries, and it is these transformations which are relevant to the subject.

Manpower utilization within an industry is also a function of long-run trends. Technological developments and changing organizational forms are the basic factors affecting occupational requirements. Examples of changes in these variables were evident in the food service industry where the development of prepared and frozen foods and the growth of chain stores were working to alter the skills required of the industry's workforce. Similarly, the health services industry will require new specialized technicians as a result of the development of new instruments and techniques, and new types of manpower will be required if the industry's organizational pattern shifts from an emphasis on in-patients to greater attention for ambulatory care. These trends have important consequences for upgrading opportunities, but they are not short-run changes that are responsive to programmatic intervention.

Manpower programs, which are efforts to improve the quality of the labor force and enhance the employability of enrollees, are not likely to have a significant affect upon the occupational structure of an industry. The relationships between the quality of the supply of labor and the nature of the demand are complex. In general, as the educational level of the population has risen employers have raised their educational requirements. It is one's relative position with respect to the educational level of the population that determines his employability at a given time, not his absolute level of education. In this sense the quality of the labor supply will affect the nature of the demand. However, in terms of occupational structures the issue is not whether an available supply of highly trained labor will be given preference over other less skilled workers for employment, but whether an expanded supply of suitably trained workers will alter the number of skilled positions for which an employer recruits. The recent experience of many well-trained teachers who cannot find employment in their field indicates that this new supply has not altered the industry's requirements. Schools could have responded to the increased supply by reducing average class size in order to absorb the available manpower, but society does not appear to be willing to meet the added costs this would require. The case of nurses is less clear cut. If many more registered nurses were trained, hospitals would have the option of increasing the ratio of nurses to aides in their nursing departments. The question is whether society would be willing to meet the added costs these changes would require. The issues are, first, how much reduced teacher-pupil or nurse-patient ratios enhance the quality of the service rendered, and second, whether society is willing to pay the increased price for whatever additional benefits are produced. In a few industries, particularly the labor-intensive service industries, there is some room for the supply of trained manpower to influence the demand for itself, but there are often tight constraints due to the need to keep costs within a range for which the consumer is willing to pay. For this reason, manpower programs are not likely to alter significantly an industry's manpower utilization pattern.

A second approach to upgrading policy accepts as given the number or proportion of better jobs available within an industry, but seeks to increase the percentage of these positions filled from internal sources. One finding of this study is that a substantial majority of these jobs are currently being filled from internal sources. Nevertheless, it may be possible to improve upon existing practices and increase the already high percentage.

The case studies point to two sets of circumstances which frequently foster the use of outside sources of manpower. First, positions which require a credential dependent upon periods of formal training are usually not suited to promotional classification. Extreme cases include physicians, business executives, lawyers, and architects. These occupations now have minimum entry requirements that specify several years of academic preparation. The length of time it would take employed workers to complete these courses of study is generally considered too great to allow for substantial numbers of these positions to be filled by upgrading. Less extreme cases include occupations such as nurses, X-ray technicians, and dental hygienists, all of which require shorter periods of formal preparation. These fields are better suited to part-time study and a greater number of programs in these areas for employed workers might make possible greater use of internal sources in filling positions.

Upgrading programs for hospital personnel wishing to qualify as practical and registered nurses have been undertaken, and there are lessons we can extract from that experience. Training co-sponsored by the New York City Department of Hospitals and District Council 37 of the American Federation of State, County, and Municipal Employees and funded by the U.S. Department of Labor has been highly successful. Of the 463 nurse aides who enrolled in the two-year program, 422 completed training. Salary gains for the graduates varied widely because the beginning LPN salary is lower than the highest steps of the nurse's aide pay scale. Aides with many years experience actually suffered a reduction in base pay as a result of their promotion, while others with less seniority improved their annual earnings by almost $1,000. Costs were high, $5,178 per enrollee or $6,185 per graduate, and were divided almost evenly between instructional costs and wage payments for released time from work.[1] Such expenses are justifiable in experimental projects designed to demonstrate the feasibility of innovative approaches, but long-run programming requires a more rational allocation of costs.

Another program intended to increase reliance upon internal sources is the Training Incentive Payments Program funded by the Department of Labor and administered by the Institute for Public Administration. Rather than providing training directly, the program reimburses employers for wage increases earned by employees chosen by the firm in consultation with the institute's staff. The hope is that incentive payments tied to wage increments will stimulate employers to undertake whatever action is required to upgrade workers. The program has had difficulty getting started. At the end of its first year only 92 workers were actively enrolled, although it is authorized to accept up to 500.[2] The fact that the project is still in its initial stages makes evaluation difficult, but its administrators feel that changes in the incentive payment structure are needed, as well as greater emphasis on consultation and technical assistance to employers, to help them design the measures needed to promote from within. The program has not yet developed a set of services which are broadly applicable and effective in altering employer staffing practices, but the limited experience indicates that incentive payments alone will not achieve this end.

Typically, when positions are filled by new entrants and formal training takes place prior to entry into the labor force, the worker bears a cost in the form of earnings foregone during training and shares in the instructional cost with tuition payments. In most institutions tuition covers only a portion of the total instructional costs and the federal, state, and/or local government pays for most of the instructional expenses. Under these conditions employers bear none of the costs of

[1] Florence Stern, "Upgrading Nurses' Aides to LPNS Through a Work-Study Program," Final Progress Report (Education Department, District Council 37, 1970).

[2] Institute for Public Administration, "Training Incentive Payments Program, First Years Operation" (New York: Institute for Public Administration, June 1, 1971).

formal training. Efforts to encourage employers to upgrade current employees rather than hire new entrants will also have to free them of responsibility for formal training costs if the programs are to be acceptable. An upgrading program able to compete with traditional training and staffing patterns will have to share costs between employee and the government. Few would argue against government assuming the instructional costs, although debate is likely over the relative responsibility of each level of government. Should the federal government provide funds for such training or should they be provided as part of the regular services of local institutions or should there be some sharing of instructional costs among federal, state, and local levels of government? Intergovernmental fiscal relations in the United States are undergoing a continual transformation. There are no agreed upon rules for the sharing of the costs of public functions among different governmental units, but some mutually acceptable formula for matching grants could be developed.

Responsibility for the costs of foregone earnings is even more problematic. Under traditional training patterns the future worker bears all of this cost, usually because he believes it will be more than recovered through increased future earnings. This argument might also be applied to employed workers. Then all that is required of government is the financing of part-time training opportunities and, perhaps, loans to support the worker and his family while he is sacrificing part of his income to attend classes and until he receives the returns from training. Alternatively, the training might be made available after working hours so that he is required to sacrifice leisure or sleep rather than earned income. But the assumption of an upgrading policy is that it is more desirable to have positions filled internally than externally, so the government ought to be willing to assume some added costs to produce this desired end. The issue is what fraction of the costs of foregone earnings the government ought to provide to workers in training. The obvious answer is "as much as is necessary to insure participation," but exactly what this fraction is remains to be determined. In the successful nursing program described above workers received practically 100 percent of the costs of foregone earnings. But it may be possible that if training is provided after working hours employees will be willing to sacrifice their leisure with little or no compensation. In cases where this is not possible because of the nature or the duration of the training, it remains to be determined what percentage of foregone earnings must be reimbursed in order to obtain employee participation and to what extent loans might substitute for direct payment.

It should also be pointed out that when training arrangements require the employee to be available for work only on a part-time basis, employers may be reluctant to participate because this requires schedule and staff changes as well as other disruptions during the transitional period. Since continued reliance upon external sources does not impose such burdens on him, successful efforts to increase upgrading practices should provide the employer with technical and recruiting assistance during this transition.

In sum, there is a potential to increase the proportion of better jobs filled through upgrading when these positions require formal institutional training. Taking advantage of this potential will require a program that provides publicly supported part-time training services, some payment to workers for the costs related to participation in training, and assistance to employers in adjusting their routines to a partial part-time workforce. In developing such a program it may be advisable for the federal government to bear all the costs of demonstration projects designed to test the feasibility of such approaches and thereby develop employer receptivity and to determine what level of employee support is needed. However, for long-run program commitments a rational allocation of costs among employer, local and federal government, and the employee must be developed.

The second set of circumstances which encourages the use of external sources in filling better jobs is the availability of qualified manpower in other industries. The best example in the case studies is the movement of painters, carpenters, and other craftsmen into the construction industry from related fields. Also turnstile maintainers employed by the Transit Authority were drawn from workers in private industry experienced with coin boxes, cash registers, and similar equipment. In these instances the necessary skills are not acquired in a formal or institutional setting, but depend upon work experience in which training is a by-product of the production or service process. Our studies revealed that the skills needed for most jobs are acquired in this manner. Suitable settings in which to obtain the necessary work experience may exist in more than one industry. As noted in the Introduction, the industry based definition of upgrading selected for this study has limitations. There are job progressions which cross industry boundaries. Some workers, such as the painters and carpenters cited above, increase their earnings by moving to a related occupation in an industry other than the one in which they acquired basic skills. This pattern represents advancement opportunities which ought to be considered a form of upgrading and is no less desirable than skill acquisition and occupational advancement taking place within an industry. Occupational sequences requiring interindustry shifts are not confined to white collar careers, and those movements should be recognized as an established method of securing better jobs.

An approach to upgrading which focuses upon increasing the percent of higher wage jobs filled internally offers greater opportunities for successful short-run programmatic intervention than does one which seeks to alter occupational structures. But even this approach has severely limited potential. Upgrading already supplies the manpower for many better paying blue-collar positions, so in many industries the margins for improvement are small. It is only for positions requiring formal training and released time from work that significant changes appear to be possible. Such jobs constitute only a small proportion of employment in most industries. Of the five industries examined in this study, only health services contained a significant number of suitable positions. Even in that field, they were only 15 to 20 percent of the total employment.

Two additional points should be made about the objective of increasing the proportion of better jobs filled internally. First, throughout this study the internal labor market has been defined in terms of an industry rather than the firm. If individual firms were viewed as the boundary unit of the internal labor market, it would probably be true that a far smaller percentage of the higher wage jobs are filled from within. While no data have been presented on the subject, the case studies revealed that much intraindustry advancement takes place through changes in employers. However, one must ask what the possible benefits are from increasing the degree of intrafirm advancement if no gain is made in the level of intraindustry advancement. For example, does it promote any social objective to have an employer promote his own busboy to a vacant waiter position rather than to hire a busboy with equal experience from another restaurant? As argued in the introduction, upgrading is best viewed as an industry-wide practice and the firm should be considered one setting within which upgrading may take place. In instances where gains can be made in the percent of positions filled from within an industry, it may be practical to implement suitable programs through a single firm. But programs which simply alter the practices of a single firm without improving the potential for mobility within the industry are of dubious value.

The second point to be made about increasing the proportion of jobs filled internally is that there is no generally agreed upon level of internal staffing which is considered optimal. Is the goal to have all (100 percent) better jobs filled from within? Some industries approaching this end are beginning to call the practice into question. For example, in education principals are drawn almost exclusively from the ranks of teachers and often must have professional preparation and experience as teachers. Some educational reformers have begun to question this practice on the grounds that principals recruited from other industries might be more effective in designing and implementing improvements in the public schools. Similarly, the closed system of recruitment for higher level positions in many local police departments has been indicated as a contributing factor in the alleged corrupt behavior of policemen. Whether or not any of these specific charges are true, it should be realized that external recruiting has some value in promoting innovation and accountability. This fact should be taken into consideration when upgrading goals are determined.

A third approach to upgrading accepts as given both the number of upper level jobs and the percent which are filled internally. Added to these considerations is the fact that in practically all cases the number of workers eligible for advancement exceeds the number of available positions. The important issue under these conditions is who should be selected from those eligible. The case studies provide illustrations of several principles which are followed in making the decision. They include seniority, quality of performance in lower level positions, testing of aptitudes by outside agencies, nepotism, and racial or sexual discrimination. Typically a weighted combination of factors is employed, as is the case in the Transit Authority where promotions depend upon seniority and test scores with women categorically excluded from eligibility for some positions. In most private industries selection depends more heavily upon informal evaluation by supervisors. This informal process has often resulted in discriminatory practices. For example, the Social Security data drawn from restaurants in New York City indicated that well over 80 percent of those in the highest income categories were recruited from within the industry; yet none were Negro, even though blacks constituted about 20 percent of the lower level workforce.

The problem of suitable criteria for selecting from among the pool of eligible workers is not conducive to a simple solution. Different values are reflected in each of the alternative criteria, and the question arises as to whether government action should be undertaken to promote certain values over others. Should the goal of upgrading policy go beyond increasing the level of upgrading activity to include priorities relating to whom among the eligibles should be advanced? There is no formula, such as a weighted average of test score and a supervisor's evaluation, which can be universally applied to upgrading selection, but it is generally agreed that the elimination of certain factors is desirable. If this approach is followed, upgrading policy requires efforts to eliminate the application of discriminatory principles. Certain practices in promotion and hiring decisions are already outlawed. For example, employer rules specifying that Negroes are considered ineligible for specific positions have been declared illegal. Progress is also being made in eliminating sex discrimination. Lower level federal courts have ruled against employer regulations categorically prohibiting women from jobs such as railroad agents and telephone switchmen. But even in cases where no overt policy exists, the application of other criteria may result in situations where Negroes or females are not represented at higher levels to the same degree they are at lower levels. For example seniority rules or outside testing might result in an underrepresentation of blacks even though they are not categorically excluded from consideration. The issue is whether greater weight should be attached to the goal of an

103

integrated workforce than to the values associated with seniority and general aptitude testing. Seniority rules have not been challenged on these grounds, but some testing procedures have been. Recently, the Supreme Court, in the case of *Willie S. Griggs v. Duke Power Co.*, declared unconstitutional testing practices which had discriminatory results when the tests were designed to gauge general aptitude rather than measure job performance. The Court said, "If an employment practice which operates to exclude Negroes cannot be shown to be related to job performance, the practice is prohibited." Tests must "measure the person for the job and not the person in the abstract." The Court ruled that there need not be a discriminatory intent, only discriminatory results; "Under the (Civil Rights) Act (of 1964), practices, procedures, or tests neutral on their face, and even neutral in terms of intent, cannot be maintained if they operate to 'freeze' the status quo of prior discriminatory exployment practices." This decision can lead to a re-examination of many devices now used to select from among groups eligible for advancement. If upgrading policy is defined as an effort to alter the principles used in selecting individuals for better jobs, then energetic enforcement of contract compliance regulations and the Civil Rights Act of 1964 are likely to be the most effective upgrading programs.

A fourth approach to upgrading focuses upon the composition of the manpower pool eligible for advancement, rather than the criteria used to select among them. A goal of upgrading policy may be to increase the size of the group eligible for a given position. Since we have found that in almost every case the eligible pool far exceeds the number of available positions, one might ask why efforts should be made to enlarge the group further. The reason that can be offered is expanded opportunity. Broadened opportunity has traditionally been a goal of United States social policy, even though opportunities for advancement are not always followed by advancement. By qualifying those previously excluded from consideration for advancement we are broadening access to better jobs without necessarily expanding the number of better jobs. Depending upon the criteria used to select from among the eligibles, those with newly gained access may or may not actually experience occupational gains. This approach offers potential dangers as well as potential benefits. An increase in the pool of eligibles not accompanied by an increase in the number of available positions may yield an increase in the number of disappointed and dissatisfied workers.

Efforts to broaden access to better jobs are usually undertaken as part of a program to overcome discriminatory practices. Employers may be willing (or forced) to promote according to nondiscriminatory criteria, but they find that no blacks (or females) are eligible. Special efforts are needed to prepare minority workers so they may compete for better jobs. Upgrading programs designed to expand the pool of eligible workers are described in a review of several programs by E. F. Shelley and Company. One program was operated by the Georgia Kraft Company, a firm which had traditionally hired blacks for jobs as laborers in the woodyard:

However, the 1964 Civil Rights Act declared illegal racially segregated career progressions, and Georgia Kraft subsequently modified its job ladder. The firm was then faced with the problem of raising the literacy levels of the woodyard laborers to permit them to move into higher level jobs.

Georgia Kraft then installed a U.S. Research and Development Corporation training package in the Rome and Macon facilities to provide remedial education for the unqualified workers. The program, administered by the U.S.R.&D. staff, consisted of 183 hours of programmed instruction in mathematics, reading and communications skills. The training was conducted on the employees' own time, in a special plant facility open 12 hours per day.

The entire laborer pool at the Rome mill (64 workers) was urged to apply for the training. Of these 49 indicated an interest (after a good deal of urging by the project and company personnel) and began classes. Forty-three have completed the program, and 10 of these have already been upgraded. At Macon, 50 of 53 eligibles entered the program and 30 have completed the training. Most are expected to move up as openings occur, but with a turnover rate of only 2 or 3 percent this process can be quite slow.[3]

[3] Arthur Kirsch and Donald Cooke, *Upgrading the Workforce: Problems and Possibilities* (New York: E. F. Shelley & Co., 1971), pp. 122–23.

A program with similar goals was undertaken at the Hughes Tool Company:

The company's collective bargaining agreement with the United Steel workers contains unusually graphic career maps indicating all lines of progression in each department, the priorities of consideration for filling each job vacancy, and the physical location of each specific job within each labor grade. Promotions are made on the basis of departmental seniority and testing which begins at labor grade six. All employees eligible for promotion are notified and may apply for the job.

Hughes Tool has experienced some difficulty in qualifying minority group employees for positions beyond the lower labor grades. In response to this, the company has modified a 10-week voluntary lecture course (which was originally intended to help all employees pass the test) to meet the remedial education needs of its less literate workers. Willing employees are instructed after hours on a one-to-one basis until they can pass the simple blueprint reading and shop mathematics tests. Promotions continue to be made within the provisions of the collective bargaining agreement.[4]

The result of both the programs is to enlarge the pool of workers eligible for promotion by qualifying blacks. However, neither the number of advanced positions available to the workers nor the criteria used for selection (seniority and testing) are changed. It is anticipated that the blacks with newly gained access will successfully compete with those previously qualified and eventually move up along the established path.

A final approach to upgrading specifies as an objective improvement in the working conditions of those employed at the lower levels of the occupational structure. This approach recognizes that advancement or the opportunity for advancement is only one factor which makes a position desirable. Alternative actions which might improve worker satisfaction include improvements in wages, fringe benefits, and safety conditions. In fact, programs to increase the likelihood of occupational mobility will probably have little affect upon worker satisfaction. Opportunities for promotion rank relatively low on the list of problems causing dissatisfaction among American workers. A review of upgrading

[4]*Ibid*, pp. 130–31.

opportunities in several industries conducted by E. F. Shelley and Company noted that: "A survey of worker attitudes was outside the reach of this project, but interviews with union leaders at the grass roots level—if they can be taken as fairly reflective of their constituencies' interests—revealed little or no concern with the potential for promotion in any industry."[5] Recently a survey of worker attitudes was undertaken by the Survey Research Center at the University of Michigan under contract with the Department of Labor. They found that the problems which trouble workers most relate to fringe benefits, safety standards, and pay levels.[6] Workers tend to attach less importance to opportunities for promotion. Programs designed to reduce worker dissatisfaction are likely to be most successful if they accept this scale of priorities.

Upgrading programs can be designed to achieve one or more of the following policy objectives: altering occupational structures so as to provide a greater proportion of upper level jobs; increasing the proportion of better jobs filled internally; rationalizing the criteria used to select those who are to be advanced; enlarging the pool of manpower eligible for advancement; and increasing the job satisfaction of employed workers. The specific nature of the program required will depend upon the policy objective given greatest priority. For example, a program intended to increase the proportion of positions filled internally will provide different services and enroll a different segment of the workforce than a program intended to enlarge the pool of workers eligible for promotion. A policy intending to alter an industry's occupational structure is not likely to require efforts which would be categorized as manpower programs. The first step in the formulation of upgrading programs is the specification of the policy objective to be achieved by the program. At present there does not appear to be any clear delineation of the objectives of federal upgrading policy; programs have been funded which serve a variety of functions but do not have

[5] William Grinker, Donald Cooke, and Arthur Kirsch, *Climbing the Job Ladder: A Study of Employee Advancement in Eleven Industries* (New York: E. F. Shelley & Co., 1970), p. 18.

[6] Neal Herrick and Robert Quinn, "The Working Conditions Survey as a Source of Social Indicators," *Monthly Labor Review* (April, 1971), pp. 15–24.

explicitly stated goals. There are several programs, but there is no policy.

UPGRADING AND NEW CAREERS

The failure to identify policy goals and the confusion of upgrading objectives with other measures is apparent in the "New Careers" approach which has attracted much attention in the past few years. This approach has developed into an ideological movement, and there now exists an abundant literature on the subject, as well as a New Careers Institute and Newsletter to help promote the faith.[7] While initially intended to apply only to public services, the concept is now advanced for implementation in private industry as well. As a recent *New Careers Newsletter* proclaimed, "the model can be applied to industry, with modifications, and success achieved as measured both in terms of gains to the employee in increased wages and mobility, to the employer in increased productivity and consequent profits, and to both in sharply reduced training time and turnover."[8]

The New Careerists present a program which includes specific measures to facilitate the use of internal sources in staffing higher level positions, such as job restructuring and released time for training, but which also contains policy measures not directly related to this objective. Among the latter are expanded public service employment, unionization and collective bargaining for workers lacking these benefits, and worker and consumer participation in managerial decision-making. While each of these can be supported (or attacked) on its own grounds, the connection between such measures and the additional use of upgrading practices by employers is assumed by the New Careerists. The compatibility of these policy measures is an interesting area for re-

[7]The basic book on the subject is Arthur Pearl and Frank Riesman, *New Careers for the Poor* (New York: Free Press, 1965). Other book-length works are Frank Riesman and Hermine Popper, *Up From Poverty* (New York: Harper & Row, 1968), and Mark Haskell, *The New Careers Concept* (New York: Praeger, 1969). A popular source of information on new careers philosophy and programs is the "New Human Services Newsletter" (formerly "New Careers Newsletter"), published by the New Careers Development Center of New York University.

[8]"New Careers Newsletter" (Fall 1970).

search and debate, but it must be recognized that they are not all integrally linked to upgrading practices.

Examples can be given to support a variety of propositions. Those who feel there is an inevitable link between unionization and upgrading frequently point to the case of New York City hospital workers where highly active unions have created training funds which provide opportunities for aides and orderlies to qualify for nursing and other technical positions. But one must also note that the professional associations serving as collective bargaining agent for registered nurses have taken positions which would tighten entry qualifications for their profession by requiring college preparation and thus restrict upgrading possibilities. A less subtle example to support the opposing point of view is found in the construction industry. Several trade unions have refused to endorse or participate in new programs designed to upgrade workers with limited skills into craftsmen positions through training outside of the traditional apprenticeship route.

There may be no necessary connection between job creation in the public sector and the introduction or expansion of upgrading in service agencies. One recent study indicates that such measures do not alter entrenched promotion criteria. A report by the National Committee on Employment of Youth (NCEY) on *Career Mobility for Paraprofessionals in Human Service Agencies* concluded that "opportunities for genuine career advancement for paraprofessionals are either severely limited or completely nonexistent." The same report added the following observation: "During the early stages of the NCEY training program many people hoped that the very presence of paraprofessionals on the job, demonstrating their performance and ability at high levels, would induce changes in long-established promotion policies of agencies in human services. It was disappointing to find that even the newer voluntary agencies, unbound to adhere to established standards, chose to do so anyway."[9]

The relationships between greater worker and consumer participation in decision making and unionization and upgrading are not clear cut either. New York City's experience with experimental school dis-

[9]Washington: U.S. Dept. of Labor, E and D Findings No. 8, 1969 pp. 113-14.

tricts indicates that in the case of education community control and unionization are not necessarily compatible goals. More recently consumer representatives have opposed the upgrading system established by the Board of Education in New York City whereby teachers are promoted to supervisory positions on the grounds that more new entrants to the system are needed at all levels.

The point of all these examples is simply that one must distinguish measures intended to expand upgrading practices from other policy measures. Steps designed to facilitate occupational mobility are not identical to, and may not even be compatible with, the actions required to expand public service employment, promote unionization, and/or stimulate worker and consumer participation in institutional decision-making.

The failure to distinguish between the concepts outlined above leads the New Careerists to confuse policy objectives and to overestimate the benefits which are likely to result from implementing their ideas. If upgrading is identified with greater expenditures for public services and broader participation in decision-making, then the objectives these measures are intended to achieve and the benefits associated with these changes tend to be attributed to upgrading. Therefore, it is argued that expanded upgrading practices will improve the quality of public services, increase worker productivity, reduce welfare rolls, and will serve as a general instrument of broad social change. One must repeat that upgrading, as a useful concept, refers only to the use of intraindustry personnel for staffing higher level positions. It must be distinguished from programs of job creation which provide jobs for the unemployed or for welfare recipients, but which need not incorporate career ladders. It must also be distinguished from movements designed to achieve wider representation in the governing of institutions affecting the lives of ghetto dwellers.

Nor does upgrading necessarily result in higher quality services or greater productivity. Some sobering evidence has recently emerged from the Martin Luther King Jr. Neighborhood Health Center, a pioneering OEO project in the South Bronx. Its *Third Annual Report* states the following with respect to the aims of providing quality services and advancement opportunities:

It has become clear that all of the goals listed above cannot be fully met, and that conflict between them is inherent in the operation. Efficient services and the employment of inexperienced community residents is one of the areas of conflict. Community residents are widely employed throughout our staff. In many areas, supervisory staff has been upgraded from amongst our original cadre of trained community residents. This emphasis on training and upgrading has resulted, however, in lowered efficiency, increased costs and poorer replicability than would have resulted had we not made this attempt.[10]

Expanded and higher quality services, increased productivity, reduced unemployment, and more democratic institutions are all desirable ends. But they are generally unrelated to staffing patterns and are not the objectives towards which upgrading programs should be directed. One can argue for public service employment programs in order to reduce unemployment, for community control of local institutions in order to make them more responsive to client needs, and for new delivery systems in order to improve the quality of public services. But one cannot argue for expanded upgrading practices on any of these grounds. The aims of upgrading programs should be limited to the five objectives described earlier.

PRIORITIES AND POSSIBILITIES FOR UPGRADING PROGRAMS

In the first section of this chapter five possible objectives for upgrading policy were described. It was pointed out that the specific actions required to achieve each of the separate goals were different and that the potential for successful intervention varied among the objectives. The formulation of upgrading programs ought to take into consideration the importance attached to each goal and the probability of achieving each. By weighing priorities and possibilities we can suggest guidelines for future action.

Important as they are, the goals of increasing the number of better positions available and of increasing worker satisfaction are not likely to be achieved through manpower programs. The forces having greatest

[10]Martin Luther King Jr. Health Center, December 1969, p. 5.

influence upon occupational structures are long-run technological developments and organizational changes. Public and private research and development are likely to have the greatest payoff, not investment in the labor supply. According to the survey results and statements of union spokesmen cited earlier, the job satisfaction of rank and file workers is not significantly affected by opportunities for advancement. Training programs are not assigned a high priority by these groups. Improving work satisfaction is largely a matter of wages, fringe benefits, and safety procedures. To the extent that promotion affords these benefits, upgrading efforts can be effective. But promotions can be given to only a few and most workers want some concrete gains rather than just a chance to compete for advancement. If the problem of worker dissatisfaction is assigned high priority by policy makers, resources should be devoted to programs having a greater and more direct impact than those designed to enhance the prospects for occupational mobility.

Manpower programs can be used to increase the reliance upon internal sources in recruiting skilled manpower. However, there are only limited areas in which this strategy is applicable. Successful implementation requires careful selection of occupational categories, for few positions offer potential for intervention. But in cases where change appears possible, such as the recruitment of nurses, health technicians, and skilled food service personnel, the provision of part-time training and appropriate scheduling of working hours may help lower level workers in the industry advance.

Enlarging the pool of workers eligible for advancement and eliminating discrimination in hiring and promotion decisions provide the greatest potential for government action. Contract compliance enforcement and legal action are the essential elements in this policy. But they can be supplemented with training programs aimed at qualifying minorities for advancement so that once discriminatory barriers are eliminated there will be an available supply of candidates. Examples of the kinds of programs required to supplement legal action were presented earlier. In the Georgia Kraft case basic education courses in reading comprehension and mathematics were provided. Laborers at the Hughes Tool Company required specific skills such as blueprint reading in order to be eligible for advancement. Specially tailored programs designed to qualify for advancement minority workers concentrated in job titles formerly considered ineligible for promotion are a way to expand the opportunities for occupational mobility.

The greatest potential for intervention to improve the process of occupational mobility does not rest in efforts to raise the number of workers who are upgraded. Successful action is more likely if the goal is to enlarge the pool of workers who are eligible to compete for advancement and to prevent racial and sex discrimination from influencing the competition. Close coordination of contract compliance enforcement and the design of upgrading programs would help concentrate expenditures in the places where they are likely to be most useful. Undertaking programs of this nature requires a commitment to the value of equity, not necessarily efficiency. It is in this light that we should approach upgrading policy.

Soc
HD
5715.2
B74

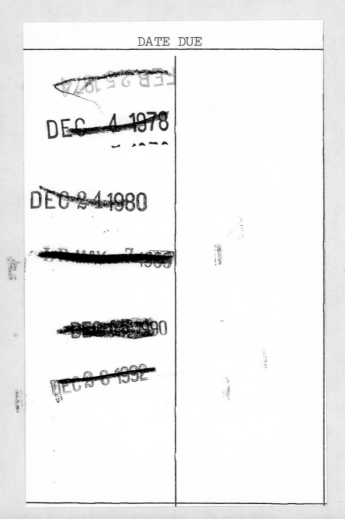

DATE DUE

FEB 25 1974

DEC 4 1978

DEC 2 4 1980

MAY 7 1985

DEC 13 1990

DEC 8 1992